UNION INTERNATIONALE DES SCIENCES PRÉHISTORIQUES ET PROTOHISTORIQUES
INTERNATIONAL UNION FOR PREHISTORIC AND PROTOHISTORIC SCIENCES

PROCEEDINGS OF THE XV WORLD CONGRESS (LISBON, 4-9 SEPTEMBER 2006)
ACTES DU XV CONGRÈS MONDIAL (LISBONNE, 4-9 SEPTEMBRE 2006)

Series Editor: Luiz Oosterbeek

VOL. 38

Session C76

Antiquarians at the Megaliths

Edited by

Magdalena S. Midgley

BAR International Series 1956
2009

Published in 2016 by
BAR Publishing, Oxford

BAR International Series 1956

Proceedings of the XV World Congress of the International Union for Prehistoric and Protohistoric Sciences / Actes du XV Congrès Mondial de l'Union Internationale des Sciences Préhistoriques et Protohistoriques
Antiquarians at the Megaliths. Vol. 38, Session C76.

ISBN 978 1 4073 0439 7

© UISPP / IUPPS and the editors and contributors severally and the Publisher 2009

Outgoing President: Vítor Oliveira Jorge; Outgoing Secretary General: Jean Bourgeois
Congress Secretary General: Luiz Oosterbeek (Series Editor)
Incoming President: Pedro Ignacio Shmitz; Incoming Secretary General: Luiz Oosterbeek
Volume Editor: Magdalena Midgley

Signed papers are the responsibility of their authors alone.
Les texts signés sont de la seule responsabilité de ses auteurs.
Contacts : Secretary of U.I.S.P.P. – International Union for Prehistoric and Protohistoric Sciences
Instituto Politécnico de Tomar, Av. Dr. Cândido Madureira 13, 2300 TOMAR
Email: uispp@ipt.pt   www.uispp.ipt.pt

The authors' moral rights under the 1988 UK Copyright,
Designs and Patents Act are hereby expressly asserted.

All rights reserved. No part of this work may be copied, reproduced, stored,
sold, distributed, scanned, saved in any form of digital format or transmitted
in any form digitally, without the written permission of the Publisher.

BAR Publishing is the trading name of British Archaeological Reports (Oxford) Ltd.
British Archaeological Reports was first incorporated in 1974 to publish the BAR
Series, International and British. In 1992 Hadrian Books Ltd became part of the BAR
group. This volume was originally published by Archaeopress in conjunction with
British Archaeological Reports (Oxford) Ltd / Hadrian Books Ltd, the Series principal
publisher, in 2009. This present volume is published by BAR Publishing, 2016.

Printed in England

BAR titles are available from:

        BAR Publishing
        122 Banbury Rd, Oxford, OX2 7BP, UK
EMAIL   info@barpublishing.com
PHONE +44 (0)1865 310431
  FAX   +44 (0)1865 316916
        www.barpublishing.com

TABLE OF CONTENTS

Antiquarians at the megaliths: Introductory thoughts 1
Magdalena S. Midgley

Chronicle of megalith research in the Netherlands, 1547-1900:
    from giants and a Devil's Cunt to accurate recording 7
Jan Albert Bakker

Jean-Marie Bachelot de la Pylaie (1786-1856). The journey of an archeologist
    among the antiquaries in Brittany in the second half of the XIXth century 23
Serge Cassen and Cyrille Chaigneau

The V*idedys* long dolmen 1643-2006 31
Torben Dehn

Research history of the Altmark megalithic tombs 37
Barbara Fritsch

Nineteenth-century Portuguese at the megaliths 45
Ana Cristina Martins

William Greenwell and the diversity of antiquarianism 51
Jeff Sanders

The Lukis family of Guernsey and the study of megaliths in the 19th century 59
Heather Sebire

Antiquarians at Swedish megaliths 67
Karl-Göran Sjögren

LIST OF FIGURES

Fig. 1.1. Megalith at Katelbogen, Mecklenburg 2

Fig. 1.2. Engraving from J.H. Nünningh *Sepulchretum gentile* (1714) showing, in the background, a North German passage grave totally devoid of a covering mound 3

Fig. 2.1. The Rolde hunebeds as 'COLUMNAE HERCULIS, *Duvels Cutz hodie*' on the oldest palaeographic map of the northern Netherlands, called 'The situation of ancient Frisia under Emperor Augustus, as indicated by the sources'. Inset of a map of Friesland-Groningen by Sibrandis Leo in *Theatrum Orbis Terrarum* of Ortelius, Antwerp, edited in 1579 and following years. The reproduction is from the 1595 edition, which gives J. Hopperus's name for the first time 9

Fig. 2.2. Johan Picardt 10

Fig. 2.3. Giants and hunebeds: a) Giants at the hunebed with one giant munching a bearded man; b) Giants building a hunebed, while normal-sized men are looking on contemplatively. Heraldic Herculesses or 'savage men' with clubs seem to have influenced the appearance of the actors 11

Fig. 2.4. Titia Brongersma, dressed as Sappho or a Greek Muse, supervises the excavation of hunebed D27-Borger. The depiction is a complete fantasy as the excavation took place in the chamber, not outside. For lack of better images of hunebeds it was reproduced by Keysler and by Stukeley, without persons 12

Fig. 2.5. a) H. Dryden is surveying the Great Hunebed D27 at Borger, 13 July 1878 (seen from the north). Pencil drawing by W.C. Lukis aided by a camera lucida; b) plan of hunebed D15-Loon by H. Dryden, ink and watercolour 18

Fig. 3.1. Bachelot's drawings of several megalithic sites (Saint-Nazaire passage grave with form of its cairn – now inside the city; Crozon alignment – destroyed; Kerbourg passage grave with the form of the cairn; Pierre Fendue alignment in the Brière marshland – destroyed) 24

Fig. 3.2. Drawing by Bachelot of Carnac alignments: view from the Manio "giants" and "quadrilatère" remains in the direction of St-Michel tumulus (with a double edifice on the top); on the left Kermaux windmill and, in the centre, Kermario lines. Synoptic Chart presents an attempt at the classification of Celtic monuments 26

Fig. 4.1. The megalithic tombs on each side of the rails in Birkede Skov: a) Kælderbakken in 1887 and b) Langben Rises Høj in 2005 32

Fig. 4.2. Illustration from O. Worm: *Danicorum Monumentorum Libri Sex*, 1643 32

Fig. 4.3. Illustration from E. Pontoppidan: *Den Danske Atlas I*, 1763 32

Fig. 4.4. a,b,c,d,e: Videdys. The National Museum's survey from 1887 and
photograph after restoration in 1937, plus two photographs from 2005 33

Fig. 4.5. Here lay the long barrow Kælderbakken until 1887 when it was used
as fill under the railway tracks 35

Fig. 5.1. Geographical situation of the Altmark 38

Fig. 5.2. Distribution of megalithic graves and Neolithic settlements
in the Altmark (triangle: megalithic grave, circle: settlement) 38

Fig. 5.3. Megalithic graves of Diesdorf (I and II), Hasselt (N. III) and Bretsch
(IV and V), published by Gerike 1751 (Bekmann / Bekmann 1751, table II);
only Diesdorf II (Salzwedel) is still preserved 39

Fig. 5.4. J.F. Danneil's megalithic travel route in the Altmark, 23rd June
to 12th August 1842 40

Fig. 5.5. E. Krause und O. Schoetensack during their researches in Lüdelsen,
Altmarkkreis Salzwedel 41

Fig. 6.1. Royal Decree of 1721 46

Fig. 6.2. Headquarters of the Royal Association of Portuguese Archaeologists 47

Fig. 6.3. Portuguese megalith published in the second half of the 19th century 48

Fig. 6.4. Engraved plaques from dolmens excavated during the 19th century 49

Fig. 6.5. Front page of the first inventory of ancient monuments published
in 1881 by the Commission for National Monuments 49

Fig. 7.1. "Death and the Antiquary", early 19th century satirical caricature
by Thomas Rowlandson depicting antiquaries on the occasion of the
opening of the tomb of King Edward I in Westminster Abbey 52

Fig. 7.2. "An Arch Druid in His Judicial Habit": an illustration from
S.R. Meyrick and C.H. Smith publication of 1815 *The Costume
of the Original Inhabitants of the British Isles* 53

Fig. 7.3. An "urn" from the Kilmartin Glebe cairn included
in Greenwell's 1877 publication "British Barrows" 54

Fig. 7.4. Greenwell's plan of Grime's Graves quarry site 56

Fig. 8.1. Lukis recording excavations at Le Creux des Fées, Guernsey,
in 1840 © Guernsey Museum and Art Gallery 60

Fig. 8.2. Drawing of the carvings on the interior props at Gavr'Innis,
Morbihan by J.W. Lukis © Guernsey Museum and Art Gallery 62

Fig. 9.1. The distribution of dolmens and passage graves in Sweden 68

Fig. 9.2. Hilfeling's drawing of the passage grave Hjelmars rör in 1789,
compared to a photo of the monument from 1932 72

Fig. 9.3. Hilfeling's drawing of the passage grave at Dala gärde, as redrawn
in 1791 (above), compared to the etching by Elias Martin published
by Tham in 1799 (below) 73

Fig. 9.4. Drawing of Odin's grave by Lindgren 1805 74

Fig. 9.5. Drawing of Åsahögen (Bruzelius 1822). 1A and B show the tomb
before and during excavation; 1C is another tomb, at Fjelkinge in Scania;
his Figs 11-17 show amber beads and 18-21 TRB pottery from Åsahögen 76

ANTIQUARIANS AT THE MEGALITHS: INTRODUCTORY THOUGHTS

Magdalena S. MIDGLEY[1]

School of History, Classics and Archaeology, The University of Edinburgh, High School Yards,
Infirmary Street, Edinburgh EH1 1LT, Magda.Midgley@ed.ac.uk

Abstract: Megaliths are among the most dramatic and enticing prehistoric structures. They feature in mediaeval documents and chronicles as well as in fairy tales and stories about giants. It is hardly surprising that from the earliest times scholars were attracted to the study of these monuments. From the 16th century onwards we find antiquarian descriptions of megalithic tombs, illustrations, notes on excavations and learned speculations about their significance; frequently such records are the only source of information on long destroyed monuments.
The papers collected here examine the antiquarian contribution to the study and interpretation of the megalithic tombs in Europe. They consider the nature of the antiquarians' approaches from the earliest antiquarian activities until the end of the nineteenth century, their concerns with the investigation, recording, illustration, preservation and protection of the megaliths, as well as their interpretations of the function of the monuments.
Keywords: antiquarian, megalith, learned societies, national identity

Résumé: Les mégalithes font partie des structures préhistoriques les plus spectaculaires et les plus attirantes. Elles apparaissent dans des documents médiévaux et des chroniques ainsi que dans des contes de fées et des histoires de géants. Il est peu surprenant que depuis les temps les plus anciens les chercheurs ont été attirés par l'étude de ces monuments. À partir du 16ème siècle, on trouve des descriptions de tombes mégalithiques écrites par des antiquaires, des illustrations, des notes sur des fouilles et des spéculations avisées sur leur signification; fréquemment ces documents sont la seule source d'information sur des monuments détruits depuis longtemps.
Les articles rassemblés ici examinent la contribution des antiquaires à l'étude et l'interprétation des tombes mégalithiques en Europe. Ils considèrent la nature des démarches de ces antiquaires, de leurs activités les plus anciennes jusqu'à la fin du 19ème siècle, leurs préoccupations concernant l'investigation, l'enregistrement, l'illustration, la préservation et la protection des mégalithes, ainsi que leur interprétations de la fonction de ces monuments.
Mots-clés: antiquaire, mégalithe, sociétés savantes, identité nationale

Megaliths are, without any doubt, the most tangible monuments of prehistoric Europe, dramatic and enticing structures with a particularly powerful presence in the landscape. Megaliths have featured in mediaeval documents and chronicles as well as in popular fairy tales and stories about giants. Later, they inspired the otherworldly sketches and paintings of the Romantic tradition – exemplified by such fine paintings as *Hünengrab im Schnee* (1807, now in the Galerie Neue Meister, Dresden) by Caspar David Friedrich or *Hünengrab im Winter* (1824/1825, now in the Museum der bildenden Künste, Leipzig) by Christian Dahl. Such images demonstrate the mystery, power and attraction that megaliths have exerted upon the imagination of scholars and artists over many centuries and, indeed, continue to do so to this day.

The "Antiquarians at the Megaliths" session of the XVth UISPP Congress in Lisbon, September 2006, was devoted to the antiquarians' study and interpretation of the megalithic tombs in Europe. As archaeologists we have long maintained an interest in antiquarianism, but this has been more with a view to establishing the origins and foundations of archaeology as a discipline, rather than as a reflection on the antiquarian contribution to a particular archaeological phenomenon. However, it was precisely the history of antiquarianism in association with the megaliths – the investigations, achievements and also, dare one say, the frustrations of the antiquaries – that inspired colleagues to consider this subject during the Congress in Lisbon. The papers gathered in this volume bring together initial considerations of antiquarian activities associated with the megalithic monuments in different countries and, we hope, will invite further debate and engagement with antiquarian researches at the megaliths both in areas represented by the present contributions as well as elsewhere.

Modern megalithic scholarship has come a long way from the earliest concerns with these structures, but we have lost none of the fascination that originally inspired the early students of these monuments. Indeed, it would be fair to say that many of us have, at one time or another, been keen to include an attractive antiquarian picture of a megalith to enhance the illustrative quality of our papers (Fig. 1.1), or to include a charming anecdotal story from an antiquarian past to brighten our own rather dry text. Moreover, since many of the megalithic monuments either have long disappeared or are badly ruined, antiquarian surveys, notes and, particularly, illustrations give us access to some of that lost knowledge as well as enlightening us on problems which may not have been posed in the past but are of concern today.

---

[1] I wish to thank all the colleagues who contributed to this volume. In particular I also wish to thank my husband Stephen, for his help with editing the papers, Dr. Catriona Pickard for help with illustrations and Muriel Masson for translating the abstracts into French.

Fig. 1.1. Megalith at Katelbogen, Mecklenburg (lithograph from F. Lisch's publication of 1837)

A few examples demonstrate this. The Mecklenburg antiquarian Friedrich Lisch (1801-1883), who published over 2300 archaeological papers, commented as early as 1861 on the different colours of the building materials used in megaliths. He considered the grey of the granite boulders, the red of the sandstone slabs and the white of the burnt flint scattered on the chamber floors as "sound colour composition...in the world of few colours" – a subject of colour symbolism which has re-entered the megalithic agenda a century and a half since this phenomenon was first raised in archaeological literature (Jones and MacGregor 2002, Steinmann pers. com. 2005). Similarly, Reverend William Lukis (see below and the contribution from H. Sabire), who investigated Dutch megaliths in 1878, thought some of the orthostats and capstones in the Drenthe hunebeds had been purposely split, but for long there was little consideration given to this matter. It is only now that we are recognising that glacial boulders were deliberately split to create the so-called "twin-stones" – pairs of stones placed within megalithic chambers in symbolically significant relationship to one another (Dehn *et al*. 1995, Midgley 2008).

Many megaliths today are dramatic ruins completely devoid of any covering materials, although the great efforts made by the builders to ensure that chambers were stable and dry suggest that, normally, they were intended to be hidden within imposing mounds. However there are also indications that some chambers, or at least their capstones, may have remained visible on the surface and that, in other cases, no mounds ever enveloped the chamber at all. Curiously, this may be precisely what was being portrayed in the early eighteenth century engraving included in Nünningh's work *Sepulchretum gentile*, published in 1714 (Fig. 1.2). This well-known illustration pictures diggers busily exploring a round mound but, visible in the background, there is a perfect North European passage grave with its capstones freely balanced on the orthostats, completely devoid of its mound. Such illustrations may well help us to consider the questions of the occasional absence of a covering mound or, perhaps, the destruction of megaliths: Did it always begin with the extraction of large stones? Did some mounds simply decay naturally? Was the earth perhaps thought of as a suitable, symbolically charged raw material? (Midgley 2008).

The antiquarians, some of whom we encounter in the following pages, were not merely investigators of megaliths but, rather, flamboyant characters who contributed in a more general way to the development of arts and sciences. There have of course been many, and not always flattering, definitions of the antiquary, for example that of a scholar with an unnatural and unhealthy obsession with the past – so eccentrically epitomised by the figure of Jonathan Oldbuck in Sir Walter Scott's eponymous novel "*The Antiquary*". But, if we allow the antiquarians to speak for themselves, then in the words of William Borlase, that keen eighteenth-century student of the ancient monuments of Cornwall:

"*The proper business of an Antiquary is to collect what is dispersed, more fully to unfold what is already discovered, to examine controversial points, to settle what is doubtful, and by the authority of Monuments and Histories, to throw light upon the manners, Arts, Languages, Policy and Religion of past Ages*".

(Borlase, W. 1769, v)

Fig. 1.2. Engraving from J.H. Nünningh *Sepulchretum gentile* (1714) showing, in the background, a North German passage grave totally devoid of a covering mound

Modern scholarship on the antiquarian tradition has favoured the well-known and exceptional scholars, such as William Camden (1551-1623) and William Stukeley (1687-1765) in Britain, Bernard de Montfaucon (1655-1741) in France or Ole Worm (1588-1655) in Denmark, accommodating them in the narrative of the emergence of archaeology (Schnapp 1996, Schnapp and Kristiansen 1999, Trigger 2006) and thereby under-emphasising the contribution of others who fit less easily into our current interpretative frameworks.

We may well put on a wry smile at the twelfth-century ideas of Saxo Grammaticus (see Sjögren's contribution), equally expounded in the seventeenth century by the Dutchman Johan Picardt, that megaliths were constructed by giants (discussed in detail in Bakker's contribution). However frivolous it seems to us today, this idea is perhaps less astounding when viewed against the background of the Middle Ages, theological literature of the times and the revival of classical writings (in which Giants strode from mountain to mountain to conquer the seats of the Olympian Gods). We should not be too harsh on the late sixteenth- and early seventeenth-century scholars for believing in Giants – after all witches figured equally on the contemporary agenda.

But there is another dimension to the study of antiquarianism: the need to place the antiquarians at the megaliths within the intellectual contexts of their times. We need to interpret the antiquarians' legacy not just for archaeology but also for history – the history of our discipline, naturally, but also their particular contribution to the cultural history of their time. As the papers gathered here demonstrate, there are similarities, as well as contrasts, to be observed between the different approaches of antiquaries across Europe – in Britain, France, Portugal, the Netherlands, Germany and Scandinavia – since much of this work was conducted in a spirit of searching for and defining a deep national past.

The antiquarians' thirst for knowledge made them energetic researchers, travelling the countryside searching for ancient artefacts and fossils, excavating barrows, writing to each other, exchanging information, deriving evidence from unwritten records. Their interest in the material aspects of the past – artefacts, ruined structures, earth works – was made to yield up the secrets of that past.

One asset was, of course, the network of antiquaries and their co-operators (local squires, schoolmasters, parish priests, etc.) in the provinces of different countries, who wrote long letters to one another, sharing and exchanging information, creating a sort of invisible "Republic of Letters". Thus, for instance, the "wandering antiquary" Martin Friedrich Arendt (1769-1823), from Altona, travelled across many countries from Southern Scandinavia to Ireland and Italy, conveying information, carrying descriptions and new drawings from one country to another (see Sjögren's note on the transmission of Lindgren's now famous drawing of the Axvalla chamber from Sweden to France). Arendt is even known to have made a guest appearance at one of Goethe's literary club evenings in 1807 which he attended as "a specialist in Icelandic and Scandinavian literature and culture" (Heyse Dummer 1949).

A different sort of strength lay in the various learned societies which sprung up as a result of antiquarian research. Thus, the *Académie des Inscriptions et Belles Lettres* was founded in 1663 to become a leading French institution devoted to the advancement of historical, archaeological and philosophical scholarship, concerned with the study of monuments and cultures of early civilisations. The *Society of Antiquaries of London*, founded in 1707, evolved from activities of an earlier *College of Antiquaries*, and defined its purpose as the study of antiquities, particularly as they related to the history of Great Britain. At its peak, in the early nineteenth century, the Society of Antiquaries had a membership which exceeded even that of the Royal Society (Sweet 2004).

While such national societies attracted a membership of illustrious gentlemen from the aristocracy, landed gentry and influential politicians, the most active antiquaries emerged from the professional classes and many of them carried out important work on a regional level. Thus regional associations such as the *Gesellschaft für pommersche Geschichte und Altertumskunde* operating from 1825 in Western Pomerania (Pomeranian Historical and Antiquarian Society) or *Die Königliche, Schleswig-Holstein-Lauenburgische Gesellschaft für die Sammlung und Erhaltung vaterländischer Alterthümer* (The Royal Society of Schleswig-Holstein-Lauenburg for the Collection and Preservation of National Ancient Monuments and Artefacts) provide excellent examples of provincial societies which played as significant a role as those at a national level (Schlette 1985, Jöns and Lüth 2001).

These various societies provided the antiquaries with an identity and a forum for discussion and exchange of ideas, brought them into the company of like-minded individuals, and spurred them – sometimes in a spirit of strong competition – to write pamphlets, accounts of local histories, etc. While some had literary gifts – we need only browse through the *Notes* of Prosper Mérimée to appreciate the eloquence of his writing (Auzas 1971) – others wrote in excessively laborious and detailed fashion, with appendices and lengthy footnotes. Indeed, we can thank the antiquaries for introducing the footnote at the bottom of the text – as, apparently, they had no great qualms about disrupting the aesthetic appearance of a page (Sweet 2004).

It is very striking that antiquaries, many of whom exuded enthusiasm for the megaliths and who devoted time and energy to their investigations, were individuals of many interests and very broad learning. They were naturalists, men of letters, priests, schoolmasters or businessmen; some indeed combined many interests within their person. We may well wonder how these individuals found the time for all these activities but, more significantly, they serve to remind us – professional archaeologists as we are – that we do not have a monopoly in archaeology, a point worth remembering when we tackle the interpretation, preservation and presentation of monuments to the general public.

Thus the seventeenth-century antiquarian Edward Lhwyd (1659/60?-1709), who was an unpaid keeper of the Ashmolean Museum in Oxford, apart from megaliths and other local antiquities had a great interest in fossils and was responsible for producing the very first catalogue of fossils and minerals in Britain; the engravings which accompanied the catalogue were particularly useful, as they permitted an easy recognition of types and could be used in the field. Another, William Borlase (1695-1772), a priest with several parishes to attend to in Cornwall, was a great student of the natural history of the area (especially minerals and fossils, his collection of which he donated to the Ashmolean Museum) and an antiquarian who described the antiquities of Cornwall in 1754. Jean-Marie Bachelot de la Pylaie (1786-1856), whose forgotten archaeological contributions are highlighted in this volume by Cassen and Chaigneau, was known first and foremost as a botanist; and that other great naturalist and classifier, Carl von Linné (better known as Linnaeus) also concerned himself with megalithic tombs in his travels across the Swedish provinces (see Sjögren's paper).

Of the archaeological dynasty created by Frederic Corbin Lukis of Guernsey, several of Lukis' sons distinguished themselves in the field of archaeology (see the contribution by H. Sebire). They all had wide-ranging interests which included, among other fields, engineering, medicine, geology, natural and ecclesiastical history. Lukis' daughter Mary Ann employed her artistic talents in illustrating her father's work. We only need to remind ourselves of the extraordinary contribution made by Lukis' third son, Reverend William Collings Lukis – together with his archaeological companion Sir Henry Dryden of Canons Ashby – who made extensive plans and notes on the megalithic monuments at Carnac, Brittany and in Drenthe in the Netherlands. Importantly, both projects were carried out prior to the reconstructions which were undertaken in the latter part of the nineteenth century, and they thus provide unique records of these megalithic sites before their appearance had been altered (Bakker 1979 and this volume).

Many antiquarians were men of letters. The English antiquary John Aubrey (1626-1697) was not only the discoverer of Avebury and author of *Monumenta Britannica*, which contained the results of his work at Avebury and Stonehenge, but an early biographer. His work, known as *Brief Lives* and published posthumously, is an outstanding contribution to the development of the biographical genre, giving us insights into the most celebrated scientists, politicians, writers and aristocrats of his time (Aubrey, Penguin Edition 2000).

Another celebrated antiquarian with an interest in megaliths, perhaps one of the great truly "European antiquarians", was Anne-Claude-Philippe Tubières de Grimoard de Pestel de Lévis, Comte de Caylus (1692-1765). Born to a very old and noble French aristocratic family, he benefited from all the aristocratic privileges: wealth, friends, acquaintances and all the important social connections; he was close to the painter Antoine Watteau, and a major enemy of Diderot. Caylus was also, apparently, thoroughly familiar with the less reputable forms of contemporary Parisian life and wrote many witty stories covering those subjects.

He travelled widely in different countries, collected objects of art and wrote extensively on Greek, Roman, Egyptian and Etruscan antiquities, importantly using mundane objects and not just "great works of art" to develop his ideas of art and history. Against the background of his aristocratic origins, Caylus' antiquarian studies were marked by a wholly new spirit of modesty and free enquiry, stressing the tentative nature of his conclusions (Schnapp 1996).

Antiquarians had a vested interest in the preservation of ancient monuments. The final decades of the eighteenth and the first half of the nineteenth centuries were very important, not least on account of the spirit of the age which we know as Romanticism. Apart from poetry, literature and art, there was a strong realisation of the concept of national history which, naturally, went hand in hand with national identity – identity which was seen as being embodied in national monuments.

Ancient monuments – including megaliths – were seen more and more as the property of the nation as a whole, and thus the state could be called upon to preserve them. This is not the place to discuss the various protection laws passed in different countries, but we should note that Sweden and the Netherlands were vastly ahead of other countries in passing protection laws in 1666 and 1734/35 respectively. It is also interesting to note that, by the 1830s in France, for example, the preservation and conservation of the nation's antiquities became the responsibility of a civil servant – the Inspector of Historic Monuments.

It was in this capacity that the very flamboyant figure of the first *Inspecteur Général des Monuments Historiques de France* is known to us: we refer, of course, to Prosper Mérimée. Just like his already mentioned antiquarian predecessors, Mérimée combined many occupations: he studied law but entered the public service to become an administrator. He was an authority on mediaeval architecture, and we should perhaps regard him as an archaeologist rather than an antiquarian. His reports on the French megaliths, especially in the west of France, are well known and consulted to this day, but he was also a novelist (author of *Carmen*, which inspired the libretto for Bizet's opera), essayist and art historian to name but a few of his numerous accomplishments (Fonyi 1999).

At the other end of the spectrum, we must not omit to mention that curious and perhaps most illustrious investigator of megaliths, Frederik VII, King of Denmark who, among other subjects, concerned himself with the manner of construction of megaliths and even wrote a learned paper on the subject (Frederik VII 1862). Frederik was interested not merely in the construction but also in the preservation of megaliths: he is said to have bought a piece of land from a farmer in Schleswig in order to save a dolmen known as Poppostein – indeed, the dolmen survives to this day in a tiny pocket of "Danish" territory.

Finally, we should not forget the contribution made by the antiquarians to the popularisation of megaliths, whereby they became more widely accessible, be it through a broader readership or, indeed, in response to the demands of domestic pleasure travel – known in Britain, at any rate, as the topographical tour. Daniel Defoe for example, in his "*Tour Through the Whole Island of Great Britain*" first published in 1778, claimed he was not concerned with antiquities, a claim which curiously did not prevent him from borrowing many useful sections from Camden's *Britannia*. Travellers liked to look at antiquities; as William Borlase suggested, the observation of monuments of antiquity would set aside thoughts of fatigue: barrows and stone circles offered welcome diversions (Sweet 2004, 311).

It is hoped that the reader of these papers, gathered from the "Antiquarians at the Megaliths" session of the Congress, will also not suffer from fatigue. The antiquarian scholarship on the megalithic monuments, presented in the various papers from colleagues working across Europe, speaks of important contributions to the field of megalithic learning: dedication to providing comprehensive records based on field investigation, and creativity in developing concepts and ideas to explain the megalithic phenomenon. May these papers remind us that, while our investigations at the megaliths may be technologically greatly advanced, we are hardly justified in any claim to intellectual superiority over the science and contribution of the antiquarian.

References

AUBREY, J. (2000 edition) *Brief Lives*. London: Penguin Books (Penguin Classics series) [originally edited by A. Clark in 1898 and published by Clarendon Press, Oxford].

AUZAS, P.-M. (1971) ed. Prosper Mérimée, Inspecteur général des Monuments historiques de France "*Notes de voyage*". Paris: Hachette.

BAKKER, J.A. 1979, July 1878: Lukis and Dryden in Drenthe, *The Antiquaries Journal* 59, p. 9-18.

BORLASE, W. (1769) *Antiquities Historical and Monumental of the County of Cornwall.* (2nd edition), London.

DEHN, T. and HANSEN, S. 2006a, Megalithic architecture in Scandinavia. In: R. Joussaume, L. Laporte & C. Scarre (eds.) 2006 *Origine et développement du mégalithisme de l'ouest de l'Europe*, Colloque international du 26 au 30 octobre 2002, Musée des Tumulus de Bougon (Deux-Sèvres), vols 1 and 2, Niort: Conseil Général des Deux-Sèvres, 39-61.

DEHN, T., HANSEN, S. and KAUL, F. 1995, *Kong Svends Høj. Restaureringer og undersøgelser på Lolland 1991*, Stenaldergrave i Danmark, Bind 1, København: Skov- og Naturstyrelsen.

FONYI A. (1999) ed. *Prosper Mérimée: Écrivain, Archéologue, Historien*. Genève: Librarie Droz S.A.

FREDERIK VII (1862) *Om Bygningsmaaden af Oldtidens Jættestuer*, Kjöbenhavn: Berlingske Bogtrykkeri ved L.N. Kalckar, (English version "On the Construction of "Giants' Houses," or "Cromlechs" reprinted from *Archaeologia Cambrensis*, January 1862).

HEYSE DUMMER, E. (1949) Goethe's Literary Clubs, The German Quarterly 22 (no.4), 195-201.

JONES, A. & MACGREGOR, G. (2002) *Colouring the Past. The Significance of Colour in Archaeological Research*, Oxford: Berg.

JÖNS, H. and LÜTH, F. (2001) eds. *Mecklenburgs Humboldt: Friedrich Lisch. Ein Forscherleben zwischen Hügelgräbern und Thronsaal*. Schwerin: Archäologisches Landesmuseum und Landesamt für Bodendenkmalpflege Mecklenburg-Vorpommern.

LISCH, F. (1837) *Friderico-Francisceum oder Großherzogliche Alterthümersammlung aus der altgermanischen und slavischen Zeit zu Ludwigslust*. Leipzig.

MIDGLEY, M.S. (2008) *The Megaliths of Northern Europe*. London: Routledge.

SCHLETTE F. (1985) *Archäologische Geheimnisse unserer Heimat*. Berlin: Verlag Neues Leben.

SCHNAPP A. (1996) *The Discovery of the Past: the origins of archaeology*. London: British Museum Press.

SCHNAPP A. and KRISTIANSEN, K. (1999) Discovering the Past. In: G. Barker (ed.) *Companion Encyclopedia of Archaeology*, London: Routledge.

SWEET, R. (2004) *Antiquaries. The Discovery of the Past in Eighteenth-Century Britain*. London: Hambledon and London.

TRIGGER, B. (2006) *A History of Archaeological Thought* (Second Edition). Cambridge: Cambridge University Press.

CHRONICLE OF MEGALITH RESEARCH IN THE NETHERLANDS, 1547-1900: FROM GIANTS AND A DEVIL'S CUNT TO ACCURATE RECORDING

Dedicated to the memory of Jürgen Hoika, colleague and friend

Jan Albert BAKKER[1]

Bothalaan 1, NL-3743 CS Baarn, The Netherlands, bakker06@planet.nl

Abstract: This article focuses on the development of ideas about the identity and age of the hunebed builders, the way hunebeds were constructed, their protection, recording of their particulars, and discussions of the artefacts within them.[2] Megalith research in the Netherlands did not develop differently from that in surrounding countries, although the tempo and impact varied from country to country. In contrast to earlier studies, this article is not restricted to old observations and considerations which conform or lead to our current ideas,[3] but also deals with views which may now seem strange but were perfectly logical or at least acceptable in their time.[4]

Key words: antiquarians, megaliths, the Netherlands

Résumé: Cet article se concentre sur le développement des idées sur l'identité et l'âge des bâtisseurs d'hunebed, la façon dont les hunebeds étaient construits, leur protection, l'enregistrement de leurs détails, et l'explication des objets leur appartenant. La recherche sur les mégalithes aux Pays-Bas ne s'est pas développée d'une façon différente que celle des pays avoisinants, bien que le tempo et les conséquences varient d'un pays à l'autre. Contrairement à des études précédentes, cet article ne se restreint pas aux observations anciennes et considérations qui se conforment ou amènent à nos idées actuelles, mais considère également les opinions qui peuvent paraître étranges à présent, mais étaient parfaitement logiques ou au moins acceptables à leur époque.

Mots-clés: antiquaire, mégalithe, Pays-Bas

The 53 extant hunebeds and the 27 known or assumed sites of demolished hunebeds lie in the three north-eastern provinces of the Netherlands, Groningen, Drenthe and Overijssel (van Ginkel *et al.* 1999, 161, 163). The remnants of another possible megalithic tomb, U1-Lage Vuursche, lie in the province of Utrecht (Bakker 2004; 2005). The vast majority are in Drenthe. During most of its history as part of the Netherlands, Drenthe has been the poorest, most backward and most unknown region of the country. Until 1814, its government was left to decide on internal matters, more or less independently.[5] The hunebeds remained strictly a Drenthe affair until ca. 1870.

'HUNEBED'

The Dutch word *hunebed*, formerly *hunnebed* or *hunne(n)bed*,[6] consists of *bed*, meaning 'bed' or 'grave' (cf. German *Hünengrab*), and *hun / huyn / hiun*, plural and genitive singular *hunnen*, meaning 'giant' / 'giant's' / 'giants'' (Verdam 1911).[7] The interpretation of *hun* as 'giant' is attested around 1590. In this sense *hun* is long since forgotten.[8] It occurs throughout the Dutch-German language area in the names of gigantic earth works, such

---

[1] I am very grateful to Susan Holstrom for considerably improving my English. I also thank Dr. Wijnand van der Sanden, Province Archaeologist of Drenthe, who also studies the early documentation of hunebeds, and Mr Wout Arentzen, researcher of the writings of 19th-century archaeologists (and a 'close reader' of their texts and sources) for tips, additions, corrections and stimulating discussions.

[2] *Hunebedden* is the Dutch name for the megalithic burial chambers of the Funnel Beaker or TRB culture (ca. 3400-2800 BC, the hunebeds built ca. 3400-3000 BC). In English the more fluent *hunebeds* is also used. In Germany they are called *Hünengräber, Grosssteingräber, and Megalithgräber*. The German *Hunnebetten* are a special type with a kerb, usually within a long barrow (the term *Langbetten* is then clearer).

[3] Arentzen (2007) calls this 'the veneration of success' with reference to Glyn Daniel's approach (1981).

[4] For brevity's sake, I will generalise here that the hunebeds are oriented east-west (as most are) with an entrance in the middle of the southern side, and use the terms 'Stone Age*' and 'Metal Age*', 'TRB*' and 'Bell Beaker*' etc. anachronistically and with an asterisk for times when these concepts did not yet exist or had not yet acquired these names. [Cal] BC belongs also to this category.

[5] Drenthe was 40 hours away from The Hague. In 1808, the Danish ancient historian B.G. Niebuhr was hooted at and dirt was thrown at him in Meppel, a small but yet the largest town in Drenthe (Fuchs and Simons 1977, 131, citing from Niebuhr's *Circularbriefe aus Holland*, 1808). The railway stretches completed between Utrecht and Zwolle (1864), Zwolle and Meppel (1867) and Meppel-Assen-Groningen (1870) reduced the travel time to The Hague to five or six hours.

[6] Pronounced 'hünebett' and 'hönne(n)bett' in German spelling.

[7] Other dictionaries of Medieval Dutch and Medieval Lower or High German, consulted by W. Arentzen, present no other explanations of these words than those discussed here. Most rely on Jacob Grimm (1844, 433).

[8] Schele wrote in or shortly after 1589 about hunebeds in the wider surroundings of Osnabrück, Germany: "*Es sagen auch die bauren und inwoner des lands, das dieselbigen stein-hauffen der Hunen greber sein. Hune ist aber so viel gesagt als ein riese oder gigant, wie dan auch Berosus diese ertzvetter giganten nömet. Diese stein-hauffen liggen uber malkanderen gleich wie altaren, also das es scheinet, das sie ihr opfferhande darauff mussen gethan haben.*" (Schele 1589-1637, I, 18-9, transcript A. de Bakker). 'Berosus' was a hoax published by Annio of Viterbo (1498). Schele's explanation that *hune* means *Riese* (giant), indicates that this meaning was not generally understood any more. The terms *hu(n)nebedden / hünengräber* were originally used for barrows in general, as they still were in 19th-century Dutch Gelderland, Overijssel and Limburg (also *hunnenbelten, hunnenbergen*). Such place-names as *under Hyne grebern, ze Hünengreber(n), an Hunungggreberweg* and *zen haidengrebern* were used for non-megalithic barrows near Frankfurt am Main and in Breisgau, Germany between 1320 and 1475 (Sippel 1980, 145). Cf. also J. Grimm 1844, 433 (quoted in Arentzen 2006). The more rare variants *Heidengräber* and *Heldengräber* were also used in Germany, as was *Heune-*.

as Hunneschans and Hunnenborg in the Netherlands and the famous Heuneburg on the Danube south of Stuttgart in Germany.

The names *hunebedden* and *Hünengräber*, 'giant's beds' and 'giants' graves', demonstrate the general, probably pre- and early Christian belief that only giants could have built the hunebeds. The Catholic Church, however, fought against this pagan superstition and in the Christian religion giants were regarded as the devil and his daemons (Liebers 1986, 66). After the Reformation, the Protestant scholar Picardt and several others abroad, between 1660 and 1700, revived the idea that giants were the builders.

1547

The first known treatise written about Drenthe hunebeds is a manuscript of 1547, in which it is argued that the Rolde hunebeds are the Pillars or Columns of Hercules mentioned in Tacitus' *Germania* 34. Tacitus wrote: *"Common is a rumour [among the Frisians] that the Columns of Hercules are still preserved on the spot, either indicating that Hercules has been there or because we are used to ascribing magnificent things everywhere to his fame."*

In 1547, Anthonius Schonhovius Batavus, (Anton van Schoonhove, ca. 1500-1557), canon of St Donatian in Bruges, Flanders, finished a Latin treatise about the location of the Germanic tribes mentioned by the Classical authors, particularly Tacitus, whose *Germania* had been found and printed in the 15th century. Schonhovius argued that the *Columnae Herculis* of Tacitus were the pair of hunebeds at Rolde in Drenthe. He added a local legend and some other information, but disregarded the other possible explanation given by Tacitus and did not question why Germanicus would have had to sail over the German Ocean to see Hercules's Pillars while he could easily have visited them by going overland, to Drenthe. Did Germanicus expect to find the Pillars on Heligoland, perhaps? I translate freely, with abridgements:[9]

"The Pillars of Hercules can be seen at Rolde in Drenthe, and are greatly admired by visitors. For the stones, which form an enormous heap, are so large that no cart or ship could have conveyed them. Nor are there any stone quarries because the region is marshy. So, it is surmised that they were brought in by demons, which are venerated under the name of Hercules.

On the pillars rest altar stones – Italians call rocks altars as a renowned poet states (Vergilius, Aeneis, lib. I: 109) – on which the inhabitants formerly sacrificed living people, especially foreigners. Before the victims were slaughtered, they were compelled to crawl through a small passage below the altar stones, during which they were soiled by faeces and then caught.

This is still done nowadays, especially with born Brabanders, and murder frequently ensues. The passage itself is called 's Duvels Kut, which means Cunnus Deamonis (Devil's Cunt). Saint Boniface has put an end to the human sacrifices, however.

According to Plinius, Drusus Germanicus tried to visit this monument, incited by its fame, and sailed as the first Roman over the Northern Ocean in the name of Augustus. But [stormy weather] prevented him from investigating the sea and Hercules, as Tacitus tells us. I digress on these matters to correct an error in the Commentaries by Althamer, who in his explanation of these lines of Tacitus took these to be the Pillars of Hercules at Cadiz."

At the time the towns of the Southern Netherlands (present-day Belgium) were the administrative and intellectual centres of all the Netherlands under King and Emperor Charles V of Habsburg. The Rolde legend may have reached Schonhovius at Bruges through the Frisians Joachim Hopperus (J. Hopper, 1523-1576) and Viglius van Aytta (Wigle van Aytta, 1507-1577), who were prominent advisers of the Emperor.[10]

Presumably under the influence of van Aytta and Hopperus, the *Duvels kutte* appeared on maps made by the imperial cartographers Jacob van Deventer and Christiaans Groten. Some of these maps were published in *Theatrum Orbis Terrarum* by Abraham Ortelius, including the first palaeogeographic map (1570) of the

---

[9] Schonhovius's original text (1547, ed. Matthaeus I, 1698, 63-4) is: "*Sane non possum hic præterire Columnas illas Herculis, quas Tacitus* in* **Frisiis** *fuisse magna celebritate commemorat, quarum reliquiæ hoc tractu Trenterorum, hoc est in Drenta, adhuc visuntur, vico Roelden, haud procul a Coevordia, non sine spectantium admiratione. Sunt enim singuli lapides (quorum non parvus acervus est) tantæ magnetudinis, ut nullos currus, nullasque naves admittere posse videantur: neque ibi fodinæ lapidum sunt, ut loco paludoso, quare suspicio est, eos illuc a dæmonibus, qui Herculis nomine ibi colebantur, adductos fuisse. Stabant enim super columnas aræ, (saxa vocant Itali, ut quidam** inquit Poëta) quas ad aras incolæ vivos immolabant, maximeque advenas, quos prius quam mactarent, cogebant transire angustum foramen, quod sub aris erat, transeuntemque stercoribus infectabantur, ac petebant. Quod & hodie faciunt, præsertim si Brabantum nacti fuerint, unde sæpe cædes oriuntur. Foramen ipsum ob ignominiam 's Duvels Kut, hoc est, Dæmonis cunnus, appellatur. Sed immolationem sustulit D. Bonifacius. Hujus monumenti videndi causa, Drusus Germanicus fama excitus, auspiciis Augusti, primus Romanorum Septentrionalem Oceanum navigavit, teste Plinio, lib. vv. Sed, ut refert Tacitus, obstitit Oceanus in se simul & Herculem inquiri. Haec eo paulo latius retuli, ut eximatur Commentariis Althameri error; qui hunc Taciti locum explicans, has Herculis columnas pro iis accipit, quas in Gadibus ille statuit. [...].*" The notes are "* *Lib. De morib. Germanor.*" en "** *Virgil. Aeneid. Lib. I. v. 109.*" The 2nd ed. of Matthaeus, The Hague 1738, has minor changes in the punctuation. '*Cap. 34*' was added to note * and the complete note ** was added; but 'vv.' of '*teste Plinio lib. vv*' was not filled in. Manuscripts obviously circulated widely in the 16th century because Junius (1588) and Kempius (1588) quoted the hunebed story partly from it. Where the original manuscripts are kept now is unknown to me.

[10] Schonhovius's Devil's Cunt story was cited anonymously and in general terms by the German antiquarian at Bremen-Stade, Martin Mushard (ms. 1762 [1928], see Liebers 1986, 46-7).

Fig. 2.1. The Rolde hunebeds as 'COLUMNAE HERCULIS, *Duvels Cutz hodie*' on the oldest palaeographic map of the northern Netherlands, called 'The situation of ancient Frisia under Emperor Augustus, as indicated by the sources'. Inset of a map of Friesland-Groningen by Sibrandis Leo in *Theatrum Orbis Terrarum* of Ortelius, Antwerp, edited in 1579 and following years. The reproduction is from the 1595 edition, which gives J. Hopperus's name for the first time

Northern Netherlands during the reign of the Roman emperor Augustus (Fig. 2.1). This map by Hopperus shows two pillars at Rolde, with the legend 'COLUMNAE HERCULIS, *Duvels Cutz hodie*'. The pillars are similar to those in the coat of arms of the Emperor.[11]

1660

The Calvinist clergyman at Rolde and Coevorden in Drenthe, Johan Picardt (Fig. 2.2), published the first

---

[11] Claudia Liebers (1986, 22-6) missed Schonhovius's text in her excellent study of the role of folktales in German and Dutch studies of hunebeds from the time of Humanism and Renaissance until the early 18th century. Further details and possible explanations of the rather enigmatic text are given in Bakker 2002; several studies on Hopper and Viglius van Aytta by E.H. Waterbolk which I overlooked in 2002 can be found in Bakker 2004, 197ff.

Fig. 2.2. Johan Picardt (print by P. Holsteijn after a painting by H. Nijhoff, in Picardt 1660, facing p. 1 of Dedication)

history of Drenthe and surrounding Dutch and German regions in 1660, *A Short Description of some Forgotten and Hidden Antiquities of the Provinces and Lands between the North Sea, [and the rivers] Yssel, Ems and Lippe*. One hundred and twenty-five copies were made. He integrated folk-tales, constructive imagination, historic sources and archaeological monuments. He was the first field archaeologist of the Netherlands, paid attention to prehistoric landmarks and discussed *hunebeds*, barrows, Celtic fields, mottes, ring forts, denar hoards, etc. in detail. The same is true for north-western Germany (Jacob-Friesen 1954).

Basing himself on the *Old Testament,* the *Historia de gentis septentrionalibus* by the Swedish bishop Olaus Magnus (1554), and finds of gigantic bones, he argued that the hunebeds were burial vaults for giants,[12] who had come from Scandinavia and ultimately from the Near East. Picardt's plates of these giant hunebed builders (Fig. 2.3a and b) are now found in many books on the history of archaeology.

In the early sixteenth century, the German scholars Nicolaus Marschalk and Thomas Kantzow had still written that the megalithic tombs in Mecklenburg and Pomerania were built by normally proportioned men (Stemmermann 1934, 20-2; Gummel 1938, 10; 18-9). Johann von Velen, sexton of the cathedral of Münster, who investigated Surbold's House, the immense megalithic grave at Börger in the Hümmling, Germany, in 1613 (see below), and the cartographer Johannes Gigas (1620) did not say which tribe had built this tomb, but apparently did not think of giants (Gummel 1938, 16-18, 68 n. 4).

One of the last authors to propose that the megalith builders were giants[13] was de Hennin (1700). In two letters written in 1687, the Dutch scholar Jacob Tollius (1633-1696) described megalithic *Langbetten* near Magdeburg, Germany, seen on his way to Potsdam. In his opinion, they contained the remains of ancient Germans. In Potsdam he told the Elector of Brandenburg of these monuments. The Elector answered that he had once organized the excavation of such a megalithic tomb in Holstein with the expectation of finding the bones of giants, but that only ancient coins were discovered (Schulz 1959).[14] The editor of Tollius's letters of 1687 in the beautifully illustrated *Epistolae itinerariae* (1700, published posthumously), Henricus Christianus de Hennin (1658-1703), professor at the University of Utrecht, referred to Picardt (1660) in his notes and added a plate of giants building a hunebed, which was clearly based on that of Picardt's.

1685-1720

In July 1685, the same year that the Edict of Nantes was revoked, an *allée couverte* was investigated at Cocherel near Évreux, west of Paris. The excellent excavation report was not published for another 34 years.[15] In 1719, Bernard de Montfaucon concluded from the stone, flint and bone implements and pottery found in the tomb: *"It seems that the barbarians there used neither iron nor copper, nor any other metal"* – which tallied with the surmise of Classical authors that there was a succession of stone – copper – iron used for weapons and tools in prehistory.[16]

---

[12] Concerning giants Olaus was inspired by the *Gesta Danorum* of Saxo Grammaticus (around 1200). Like him, Picardt meant postdiluvial giants.

[13] Klindt-Jensen (1975, 35-36) mentions an even later belief in giants as megalith builders in Denmark: in a report of 1727 and of P. Syv in 1787. A certain Boymans defended the giant builders' theory in *Gazette van West-Vlaandren en Brugge*, 1819, nr 119 (Westendorp 1822, 6, 77-78, 166). Probably he was the last defendant – before 'New Age'.

[14] The second wife of the Elector, Dorothea von Holstein-Glücksburg, may have enabled this excavation, as Schulz suggested.

[15] On July 11, 1685, a legal document was drawn up which extensively describes the situation to ascertain that no Christian burials were involved. For a modern translation from T. Michel, *History of the city and county of Vernon,* 1851, see http://giverny.org.archeos/cochergb.htm. The *Syndicat d'Initiative* calls it the 'First archaeological discovery in the world', which is absurd. Johann von Velen wrote a detailed report (1613) of his excavation in Surbold's House, an enormous *Hünengrab* in Germany (see above). Admittedly, he paid little attention to the artefacts in this tomb, and in a nearby one he found 'nothing other than pieces of old pots and pans', which he sent to his superiors (Gummel 1938, 17).

[16] On Cocherel, Schnapp 1993, 268-9 and (translation of Lucretius) 332-3. The classical authors mentioned are Horatius I, *Satyr.* 3, v. 99ff; Lucretius, *De Rerum Naturae* 5, v. 1284ff; Hesiodus I, v. 150. Their

Fig. 2.3. Giants and hunebeds: a) Giants at the hunebed with one giant munching a bearded man (Picardt 1660, facing p. 23); b) Giants building a hunebed, while normal-sized men are looking on contemplatively. Heraldic Herculesses or 'savage men' with clubs seem to have influenced the appearance of the actors (Picardt 1660, facing p. 33)

On June 11, 1685, Titia Brongersma (born ca. 1648), a poetess from Groningen, called Sappho and 'musarum certe decima' by her admirers, spent the Whitsun days with her family at Borger in Drenthe. At the request of her Groningen friend, the doctor medicus, antiquarian and playwright Ludolph Smids (1649-1720), she and her cousin Lenting organised an excavation in the chamber of the Great Hunebed D27 at Borger (Fig. 2.4).

Afterwards she wrote a poem about this tomb, without mentioning the excavation. Smids, who did not assist with the excavation, received the artefacts she recovered and a summary from her describing the street-like cobble stone layer under which were pottery, 'breaking to pieces', 'ash' (charcoal) and 'petrified' (burnt) bones, which he published (1694). He also wrote a poem about Titia's excavation (Smids 1694), to which Titia replied with

---

texts are cited by van Lier 1760, 120-2. As an appendix, Montfaucon added a study by the Swiss antiquarian J.C. Iselin, who accepted the same succession and illustrated Stone Age artefacts (Schnapp 1993, 237,

269). But Montfaucon and Iselin did not yet seem to grasp the fundamental importance of this sequence for prehistoric chronology (Schnapp 1993, 269; Stemmermann 1934, 125).

Fig. 2.4. Titia Brongersma, dressed as Sappho or a Greek Muse, supervises the excavation of hunebed D27-Borger. The depiction is a complete fantasy as the excavation took place in the chamber, not outside (print by J. Schijnvoet in Smids 1711). For lack of better images of hunebeds it was reproduced by Keysler (1720, fig. 2) and by Stukeley, without persons (*Itinerarium curiosum*, 1724: Mohen 1999, ill. p. 131)

another poem. After these three poems and a lost one by J. Mensinga,[17] no other poems concerning Dutch hunebeds appeared until 1844. Between 1844 and the year 2000 more than 40 were written.[18] In his poem and other writings Smids suggests Romans, Swabians, Saxons and Danes as the peoples interred in this hunebed. Somewhat later he cancelled the Romans.

Inexplicably, in his encyclopaedia (1711) of Dutch castles, towns and antiquities, published twenty-six years after the excavation, Smids reverts to the theory that giants built the hunebeds. This is curious, because he himself and the German archaeologist Christian Schlegel (to whom he had sent some of the bones and sherds in 1685) were well aware that the interred bones were from normally proportioned humans. Schlegel's conclusion that the hunebeds were therefore built by normal men, not giants, was published in 1701 by J.C. Olearius, leading to the rejection of the giant builders' theory by the Germans J.H. Nunningh (1713; 1714), J.H. Cohausen (1714), and J.G. Keysler (1720). Cohausen and Nunningh thought that the hunebeds were built by ancient Germans who were of normal stature but more robust than modern-day Germans. They would have used wooden rollers and sticks to move the boulders.

Keysler (a member of the Royal Academy of London who had a good overview of west European archaeology) ascribed the hunebeds to the Vikings, which, given the geographic distribution of megalithic graves in western Europe, was a reasonable proposition on the assumption

---

[17] *Saxa agri Trentini, carmen*, printed in 1687. Oldenhuis Gratama, in the 1870s, and the Koninklijke Bibliotheek, The Hague, in the 1980s, could not trace it. Joh. Mensinga was a professor at Groningen. An undated manuscript *Joh. Mensinga in Terentii sex Comoedias Dictata* is in the university library of Giessen (Catalogue J.V. Adrian 1840).

[18] A poem of four stanzas by 'Extemporé' in 1844 (Arentzen 2006, 87) and one of 48 stanzas by W. Seymour Mulder in 1852 (Klompmaker, Nijkeuter & Tissing 1996, also with a selection of later poems) are excellent. A poem of seventeen stanzas with the legend of the *Langbetten* Visbeker Braut and Visbeker Bräutigam in Oldenburg, Germany (Sprockhoff 1975, nrs. 952 and 936) was published in 1801 by Pastor J.G.T. Lamprecht (Liebers 1986, 49 and appendix 7).

that all were built by one and the same people and as long as their pre-Roman* age was not recognised. This ascription was adopted by at least four authors between 1770 and 1886.[19] In his encyclopaedia (1711) Smids published, along with Titia's report, the first list of extant hunebeds. This list, partly a compilation of sites mentioned by Picardt, was inaccurate, but the existence of a large number of tombs in the north-eastern Netherlands and adjacent parts of Germany was communicated to a wider audience.[20]

1706

In August 1706, J. Hofstede and A.R. Kymmel dug a pit in the chamber of hunebed D17 at Rolde. They gave a good description of the excavated 'Roman' pottery and its stratigraphical position between different layers of stones; they mention 'ash', but no stone or flint artefacts. With a reference to Alexander ab Alexandro, lib. 3, cap. 12,[21] they inferred that pots situated higher up on a flat stone in the chamberfill had contained food and drink brought to the deceased who were buried in funeral urns deeper in the chamber. Giants were not mentioned. The objective report was not published until 1847 and had no discernible influence on subsequent studies.[22]

1730-1734

In 1730-31, the dikes and sluices along the sea in the Netherlands and Ostfriesland and Jever in north-western Germany became endangered with the arrival of the 'ship-worm', *Teredo navalis*, a wormlike bivalve mollusc brought in from Asia which attacked wood in salty waters. Most dikes along the North Sea and the Zuyder Sea consisted of 2 m wide dams of compact, non-putrefying seaweed covered by wooden fences, made of oak and pine beams, which acted as surf breakers. The beams were tunnelled by *Teredo* and broke like matchsticks. General panic ensued, because half of the country could easily be flooded!

Fortunately, the modern type of dike consisting of stone-covered earth and clay was invented within two years.[23] The result was that erratic boulders in Drenthe and parts of Germany and Scandinavia along the North Sea became valuable as building materials. Everywhere erratic boulders were taken away and hunebeds were dismantled for their stones. The removal of boundary-stones, however, prompted the Drenthe government to pass a law on July 21, 1734, prohibiting this and also protecting *"the so-called Hunebeds, which, as venerable monuments and time-honoured memorials, should be preserved everywhere"*. Undoubtedly this was due to Picardt's laudation of the hunebeds as one of the most valuable assets of Drenthe in his 1660 book, which was reprinted in 1735 and again in 1745.[24]

This 1734 law in Drenthe was the third law in the world enacted to protect antiquities. The first law was proclaimed by Christian IV of Denmark in 1620, and in 1630 Gustavus Adolphus of Sweden gave legal protection to castles, forts, dolmens, rune-stones, graves and barrows in his wide realm.[25] The legal protection of the hunebeds in Drenthe was restated in 1790. In 1809 Petrus Hofstede (1755-1839), as Bailiff of Drenthe, prohibited the smashing and transporting of stones from the hunebeds and the probing and digging for stones in tumuli. In 1818, as governor, he extended the Resolution of 1734 by ordering the local authorities *"to keep a vigilant eye on the strict compliance with this [act]... Excavation or investigation of antiquities or monuments remains forbidden without the demonstrable advance knowledge of the proper authority."*[26] The protection law was proclaimed again in 1846 and 1854.[27]

1756-1760

As a consequence of the Protection Law, Johannes van Lier (1726-1799), Fiscal-General of Drenthe, was instructed by the Drenthe government to restore (and investigate) D13, a small hunebed at Eext, which had been partly destroyed by stone-seekers, persons collecting stones for trade, in 1756. D13, which was discovered around 1726 in a barrow, had steps in the entrance on its southern side. The top of the barrow and the capstones had been taken away.

At the suggestion of his friend and former house-mate Arnout Vosmaer (1720-1799), who was director of Prince William V's famous collection and zoo, van Lier donated

---

[19] De Rhoer (1770; cf. Westendorp 1822, 125) cited by Tonkens 1795; G.W.U. Wedel (1812); Oldenhuis Gratama (1886). See also Fergusson (1872), discussed below.
[20] Most of the former is discussed in Bakker 1984. Nijkeuter (2005) gives an updated curriculum of Titia Brongersma.
[21] Alessandro Alessandri, an Italian humanist and jurist (1461-1523) published *Dies geniales* (Rome, 1522, 6 vols, repeatedly reprinted).
[22] The report is discussed in Bakker (in prep.). The copies of the manuscript give the initial S. to Hofstede, but J. is more probable. A.R. Kymmel was the new sheriff of Rolde; J. Hofstede would soon go into the Church at Ruinerwold (W.A.B. van der Sanden, pers. comm.).
[23] Straat & van der Deure, 1733; Schilstra 1974, 60-95. The heads of the vertical beams of the old wooden dike fences are visible on three drawings by Rembrandt at the Diemen sea dike: Benesch 1358 and 1172; HdG 844 (B. Bakker *et al.* 1998, 228-9; Lugt 1915, 140-2; figs. 90-3).

[24] Nordic erratic boulders were used from 1732 until 1860, when basalt from the Rhineland came into use instead. During the French occupation (1806-1813), Tournay stones from the Ardennes were used instead of the erratic boulders. The quantities and costs were enormous: between 1732 and 1802, 1.2 million tons of stone were brought to West Friesland, which was only a small part of the coastline where the dikes were renewed in the same way (Schilstra 1974, 84-87).
[25] Schnapp 1993, 176; Klindt-Jensen 1975, 27 (who called a proclamation of 1666 'the first law for the protection of monuments of Sweden and Finland'). Most of the former is in Bakker 1979b.
[26] Full texts of these proclamations, translated into English, are in Bakker 1979b.
[27] Van Giffen 1927, 38 (but see Bakker in prep., chap. 2). In 1846, perhaps in connection with the refusal of Janssen's request for permission to excavate a hunebed in 1847 (see below).

the artefacts to the young Prince's collection. He wrote five letters to Vosmaer giving his observations about the tomb and its contents, which were edited and published by the latter (van Lier 1760).[28] In the book are good illustrations of the tomb and the pottery and stone artefacts found in it. This was the first illustrated publication of TRB* artefacts in Holland. Giants could no longer be considered as builders of hunebeds, because the steps in the entrance and the height of the capstones were much too small for them.[29]

The author of this first monograph of a Dutch hunebed had access to modern literature in France and elsewhere on megaliths, on the Stone Age*, on the artefacts in them, and on the tools of primitive peoples that were discovered elsewhere in the world. Van Lier argued that some of the pottery were *urns* and had contained burnt bones, and that a [tanged Bell Beaker* flint] arrowhead would not have been made in a period when metal was current. Urns and copper artefacts in barrows and urn fields in Drenthe belonged to the Metal Age*, which preceded the Roman Period.

He thought that the hunebeds were made by the Ancient Germans, 'our ancient ancestors'. Van Lier did not discuss how the stones of the hunebeds had been brought to the site and positioned, but noted that the ancient Indians of Cusco in Peru had been able to transport much larger stones, such as one of 30 x 18 x 6 ft, across rivers (according to some without using any implements) and to build walls from them which had scarcely visible seams.[30]

At the time the composition and origin of the hunebed stones was not yet sufficiently explained. Van Lier (1760, 10) proposed that they were concretions of local sands and gravels in Drenthe. But his editor, Vosmaer, argued that the stones were various types of granite and other rocks, somewhere broken from mountains and rounded off during their transport to Drenthe by an enormous flood, either the Deluge, the Cimbrian or an unknown flood (p xiii-xix; note on p. 10-11 in van Lier 1760).

1761-1789

The renowned empirical scientist Petrus Camper (1722-1789), "a meteor of spirit, science, talent and diligence" (Goethe), whose interests ranged across a wide variety of subjects such as obstetrics, surgery, palaeontology, botany, draughtsmanship, physical features of different peoples and ancient Greek sculptures, cabinet-making and correctly formed shoes, was also interested in hunebeds.

Between 1768 and 1781, he drew eight of them, with entrances on the southern side of at least three of them (D8-Anlo-Kniphorstbos; D13-Eext; O1-De Eeze). He had a special interest in hunebed dimensions and in the volume, weight and availability of the largest stones, but almost none in the identity of the hunebed builders. His drawings were published anonymously by the Russian ambassador Prince D.A. Gallitzin / Golitsyn (1789). In the quire with these drawings[31] Camper also wrote excerpts from publications about megaliths in France (Caylus, Montfaucon) and England (Edwards), again with a special interest in the volume and origin of the stones. He also argued that much heavier stones than those used for building the hunebeds were available in the countryside, but had been too heavy for the hunebed builders to transport.

1796-1808

Adriaan Camper (1759-1820), who followed his father's footsteps and published several of Petrus's unfinished manuscripts, went on to inscribe excerpts in the hunebeds quire. Among these was one from J(e)an Potocki's *Fragments historiques et géographiques sur la Scythie, la Sarmatie et les Slaves* (Brunswick 1796),[32] which discussed the presence of Slavs to the west of the Elbe river and attributed the hunebeds in that area to them. Unlike his father, A.G. Camper took the ethnic identification of the hunebed builders very seriously and became the author of the text of the 1808 competition conducted by the Hollandsche Maatschappij der Wetenschappen (Holland Society of Letters and Sciences) in Haarlem: *"Which peoples have built the so-called hunnebedden in Drenthe and the Duchy of Bremen? In which times can it be supposed that they lived in these regions?"*

The explanatory note reveals A.G. Camper's wide international perspective: *"Because a reasoned description of the hunnebedden in Drenthe and the Duchy of Bremen is lacking, it is suggested first to compare these with kindred monuments in Great Britain, Denmark, Norway, Germany, France and Russia and second to compare the coffins, urns, weapons, ornaments, offering tools etc. from the hunnebedden with those from the burial-places of the ancient Germans, Gauls, Slavs, Huns, and other Nordic peoples about whom Pallas has noted different peculiarities."* (de Bruijn 1977, 111-2).

1809

On April 19, 1809, an intact four-capstone hunebed (D41) was discovered under a barrow at Emmen by a stone-

---

[28] Van Lier's letters were written, in 1758-1759, as a critical reaction to an anonymous publication about this tomb (1757) by H. Cannegieter (1691-1770), rector of the Arnhem Gymnasium.

[29] Van Lier 1760, 167, where he followed this observation by H. Cannegieter (1757). Van Lier discussed and rejected the giants as builders on p. 167-177. When the sources mentioned giants, heroes were meant, in his opinion.

[30] Van Lier 1760, 168.

[31] Camper (1768, 1769, 1781); Bakker 1978; 1989.

[32] The talented Polish Count Jan Potocki (1761-1815) is still famous for his *Manuscrit trouvé à Saragosse* (integral edition by R. Radrizzani. Paris: J. Corti, 1990. Dutch translation by J. Versteeg, Amsterdam 1992: Wereldbibliotheek). He also wrote several works on geography, history and political systems of other countries.

seeker. Within three days detailed cross-sections were drawn by the Government surveyor P.A.C. Buwama Aardenburg and the construction was recorded in detail by J. Hofstede (1765-1848), Fiscal General and brother of the Governor, P. Hofstede. The barrow was removed. The tomb and its contents were considered to have been made "*bien longtemps avant que le métal fût connu*". The artefacts were presented to King Louis Napoleon, in addition to J. Hofstede's collection of antiquities, which had been sent several weeks before to the Royal Museum at Amsterdam.[33]

The flat capstones of D41 were capped by flat stones and earth in order to divert rainwater and keep the chamber dry, like several megalithic tombs in Denmark (Dehn and Hansen 2006). The barrows covering most other passage graves seem not to have been higher than the base of the capstones. The capstones of D41 were flat and relatively thin, whereas the capstones of most other hunebeds were bulky and extended much further beyond the carrying stones and the barrow.[34]

1812-1822

Although he did not have a library comparable to that of the Campers at his disposal, Nicolaus Westendorp (1773-1836), the Protestant minister at Sebaldeburen in the Groningen countryside, managed to write a treatise for the Haarlem competition, for which he won the gold medal prize and 150 guilders, and his contribution was published by the Society in much reduced form in its new periodical (Westendorp 1815). He became famous and published his unabridged and extended study seven years later as a book (Westendorp 1822²).[35]

Westendorp regarded all free-standing megalithic burial chambers from Iberia to Scandinavia as hunebeds, which were all datable to the Stone Age* because of the artefacts within them. According to him, all these West European tombs were made by one and the same people, in contrast to the plural 'peoples' asked for in the Haarlem competition. Similarities in the folk-tales associated with them throughout western Europe were used to support this idea. His detailed study of the religion and religious constructions of the peoples all over the world showed him that every specific people had its own specific forms of these.[36]

To answer the main question of the competition, he carefully analysed twelve possible early peoples, including the Vikings and the Romans, and rejected all but one on the basis of what was known about the ancient relics of them. To conclude that the hunebeds were built by an unknown people "*would leave the first History of our Fatherland as dark and uncertain [as before], or a hodge-podge of fabricated fables!*" (1822, 158). The only known people who could not be rejected were the (early) Celts, who according to some older classical sources had also lived in Scandinavia and northern Germany (Cimbri).[37]

The second, enlarged edition of Westendorp's study (1822) was very positively reviewed at length by Wilhelm K. Grimm (1824) in the *Göttingsche gelehrte Anzeigen*. Grimm was convinced that ancient Germans, not Celts, had built the hunebeds. C.J. Thomsen, who was developing his Three Ages System as director of the Museum for the Nordic Antiquities at Copenhagen,[38] read this review and immediately wrote to the leading German archaeologist, J.G.C. Büsching at Breslau, in 1825, to whom he had just explained his views on relative chronology, expressing his hope "*that you will not take me for a plagiarist*", because several of his opinions were found now also in Westendorp (see Seger 1930).[39]

Thomsen considered the absolute age estimated by Westendorp much too early and was also opposed to

---

[33] The original reports by J. Hofstede were reprinted and analysed by van Giffen 1927, 28-42. The three pots illustrated by Hofstede are reproduced by Pleyte (1880, pl. V: 1-3) and van Giffen, l.c. A version by Governor Hofstede, brother of J. Hofstede, appeared as an Appendix in Westendorp's publications (1815; 1822). The artefacts from the Royal Museum and Hofstede's catalogue are now in the Leiden Museum of Antiquities.

[34] See Bakker (in press), referring to an unpublished study by J.N. Lanting.

[35] Westendorp's book (1822), inclusive Notes and Addenda, and the Appendix on D41 by P. Hofstede (which is identical to that of 1815), counted some 69000 words, more than 2.5 times those of the 1815 version, and about 655 titles were cited.
A second contributor to the contest was Georg Wolfgang Ulrich Wedel, *Erbherr auf Freudenholm bey Preetz in Holstein* (Wedel 1812). His treatise, dated July 1, 1812, discusses several archaeological finds and megalithic tombs in Holstein and their contents. It argues that the Vikings built the hunebeds. Composition, argument and scope are second to Westendorp's, and the work was not printed (HMW archives of this competition in Haarlem Archives). Some of his data, for example a description of *Langbetten* on Fehmarn, may still be important for the research in Holstein.

[36] Manuscript of 1812. Although such a survey was asked for, this section was not included in the publication of 1815 on the advice of the committee. In 1822, it returned in much reduced form (Westendorp 1882, 4).

[37] This supposition was not as absurd as it may seem now, because early authors such as Artemidorus and Plutarch had described the Cimmerians / Cimbri as Celts. This idea was generally rejected in the course of the 19th century, though recently G. Herm (1975), an author who certainly does not refrain from fantastic theories, concluded from these authors, more or less in parallel with Westendorp: 'the Teutones and Cimbri were Germans, the Germans, however, were not only an element of the large Celtic complex of peoples, as opposed to the Scythian peoples, but even the original core of it. They were the most 'Celtic' of all Celts...' (ed. 1992, 89).

[38] Since 1892 this has been the National Museum of Antiquities at Copenhagen.

[39] Westendorp thought in terms of a Stone* and a Metal Age* [a 'Two Age System' (Arentzen 2006)], while Thomsen (1836) thought of Stone*, Bronze* and Iron Age*, the well-known Three Ages system. W. Arentzen (2007, 9-13) notes that Thomsen's first letter to Büsching (February 19, 1825) did not comment on the existence of a Stone Age; only his second letter (March 1, 1825) discusses Westendorp's Stone Age*. Thus, Arentzen remarks, in this respect Van Lier (1760), followed by Westendorp (1812; 1815; 1822), was earlier than Thomsen to write about a Stone Age* preceding a Bronze or a Metal Age, based on the context of the artefacts. Thomsen's letter of July 16, 1818 to a Swedish colleague describes an embryonic Three Ages system (Klindt-Jensen 1975, 50).

Westendorp's appraisal that the pottery from the hunebeds was of high quality in comparison with later pottery. Thomsen himself considered all prehistoric pots as "coarse", although those from the hunebeds were "*admittedly, sometimes decorated with strokes and provided with rims*".[40]

Westendorp's identification of the Celts as hunebed builders was given full credence in the *Handbuch der germanischen Altertumskunde* (1836) by G.F. Klemm – a *first-rate work for its time*" (Gummel 1938, 430). But this 'Celtomania' as applied to the TRB area was soon generally repudiated. His statement that genuine hunebeds had never had a barrow would prove detrimental when 'restorations' were undertaken about 1870 in Drenthe.

1847-1869

Leonhardt Johannes Friedrich Janssen (1806-1869), curator of the collection of Dutch antiquities in the Leiden museum after a study in theology, tried throughout his life to fill in the picture of '*our most early ancestors*', the hunebed builders, as created by Westendorp. He disagreed with Westendorp that the hunebeds were built by the most ancient Celts; he thought that the earliest Germans were the builders. He visited all Dutch hunebeds in 1847 within four weeks, sketched views of them, drew schematic plans and listed them (Janssen 1848). He recognised the entrance of the hunebeds in the middle of the southern long side, but made the oval peristalithic kerbs of the tombs rectangular in his schematic plans, acting under the influence of G.O.C. Freiherr von Estorff's still famous work about the prehistoric tombs near Uelzen in Hannover (1846).

Ideas on how hunebeds could have been built gradually took shape. Cohausen (1714) had written that the hunebed stones were moved by their very strong Germanic builders on wooden rollers using sticks as levers. Westendorp (1822, 104-5) had concluded that the capstones were brought into place with the help of a ramp made of a few fir trees, wooden rollers and levers. He referred to similar earlier ideas of 'the Nordic scholars', Scandinavian or north-German authors who have not yet been identified.

In 1853 Janssen described the hunebed construction as follows: "*The simplest way of construction was this. With the help of a felled tree serving as a lever and a few truncated trees as rollers, the boulders, which were lying about, were brought together, as many as were needed for the building of a hunebed. A few people sufficed to move the stones from behind, while some in front may have drawn a rope twisted from twigs or strips of animal skin, and wound around the boulder. First, the side stones were now erected with the same lever, and mantled with earth and thus fixed; then the capstones were pushed upwards along an earthen ramp and so shifted upon the side stones. A few Drenthe hunebeds are surrounded by earth as high as the capstones, so that these tombs look as if they were just a group of flat boulders lying in a row on a hillock. Most of our hunebeds appear originally to have been surrounded by a mantle of earth on the outside to consolidate the construction. It can thus be explained how man, devoid of mechanical expedients in metal, without the aid of draught animals and not possessing the strength of giants, could make such gigantic stone constructions...*" (Janssen 1853a, 11-2).[41]

Janssen did not assume that all hunebed capstones had been completely covered by the barrow, for in 1847 several Drenthe hunebeds were still "*surrounded by earth as high as the capstones, so that these tombs look as if they were just a group of flat boulders lying in a row on a hillock*". Four years later, in 1857, the Danish King Frederik VII published an almost identical model of how megalithic tombs were built, which was published in a great number of modern languages.[42] Needless to say, Janssen was not enthusiastic about a Dutch edition of Frederik's study.[43]

ABOUT 1870

When most common heath lands were divided and given to individual inhabitants and the older laws protecting the hunebeds and barrows could not be enforced, all Drenthe hunebeds – except one – passed into the ownership of the state or the province to prevent demolition. This was due to the actions of the Drenthe lawyer, politician and amateur archaeologist Lucas Oldenhuis Gratama (1815-1887). In vain he had tried to persuade the College of Provincial States of Drenthe, in 1867, to acquire the hunebeds for the Province. The following year he

---

[40] My own copy of Westendorp (1822), which I bought at Lynge's Antikvariat in Copenhagen in 1971, carries two crossed oval and crowned stamps of the ANT. TOPOGR. ARCHIV and the pages were cut up to p. 97, which may suggest that Thomsen had tried in vain to read this wordy Dutch book. It was sold together with a great number of reprints from the National Museum (esp. from H. Kjaer, 1873-1932), including an invitation to J.A.A. Worsaae (1821-1885) to become a member of the Wiltshire Field Club.

[41] Janssen may also have read King Frederik's publication of 1853 in *Antiquarisk Tidskrift* 1852-54, 6-8, for he received the German edition of this periodical (comment from W. Arentzen). This study does not, however, yet give the essence of Frederik's 1857 publication (Bakker 1999, l.c.). Janssen added in a note to the quoted text that no animal bones had ever been found in a Dutch hunebed, but that horse bones had sometimes been found in Mecklenburg *Hünengräber*, by Lisch. The identifiable animal bones in the Hilversum fireplaces shortly afterwards (see above) therefore seemed important.

[42] M. Axboe, curator of the Prehistoric Department of the National Museum at Copenhagen, informed W. Arentzen that Janssen sent an offprint of his 1853b study to the 'Königl. Societät für Nord. Altherthümer' at Copenhagen (of which he was a member) immediately after it was printed. The offprint is stamped ANT. TOPOGR. ARCHIV and cut open, but there are no notes in the margins or other signs that it has been studied, e.g. by Worsaae or the King. The model need not have come from Janssen; it could have been largely taken from Bodiker or created with little outside inspiration.

[43] *Verhandelingen der Tweede Klasse van de Koninklijke Akademie van Wetenschappen* 1857-1865, 1862, 191-194.

published an *Open letter to the College of Provincial States of Drenthe about the care and maintenance of the hunnebedden*. Politicians, members of the Academy of Letters and Sciences and articles in several journals and periodicals showed serious interest in this matter and soon the Minister instructed the Governor of Drenthe to take action and gave him a budget.

Unfortunately, the hunebeds were also restored at Gratama's advice, without supervision of attentive observers and recorders. Following Westendorp's theory that hunebeds had never had a barrow, remnants of barrows were dug away by labourers without any scientific supervision.

In the summer of 1871, Augustus W. Franks (1826-1897), director of the Christy Collection, curator at the British Museum, president of the Society of Antiquaries of London, collector of antiquities and 'one of the best known antiquaries of his days', visited the hunebeds in Drenthe and the museums at Assen and Leiden. He saw the recent hunebed 'restorations' and sherds lying on the surface, about which he reported to the Society (Franks 1872). He made the important observation that "*the whole style of the pottery agrees with what we know from Germany and Denmark as belonging to the Stone Age*". His remark "*I ventured, while at Assen, to call the attention of the members of the Commission of the museum to the value of fragments of pottery*" makes quite clear how little Gratama and others at Assen were aware of their value.

At the Congrès International d'Anthropologie et de Préhistoire at Stockholm, in 1874, and the 1876 Congrès at Buda-Pesth, Gratama spoke proudly about the protective measures and the restorations of the hunebeds. The protective measures were highly praised, but the restorations were unanimously disapproved of by the leading megalith researchers of his day: "*One cannot restore without understanding the structure of such tombs*". It must have been clear to the specialists that Gratama had no clue about stratigraphy and artefacts.

In 1878, the Reverend William Collings Lukis (1817-1892), rector of Wath in Yorkshire and Sir Henry Edward Leigh Dryden (1818-1899), fourth baronet of Canons Ashby in Northamptonshire, who had already surveyed megaliths in the UK and Brittany, went to survey the Dutch hunebeds on behalf of the Society of Antiquaries. Unfortunately, the drastic restorations had by then already been done.

Within three weeks Dryden made painstakingly detailed ground plans and elevations of 40 hunebeds, i.e. three quarters of those present (Fig. 2.5b). Aided by a camera lucida, Lukis drew views of these monuments (Fig. 2.5a) and described their form and geographical situation. Lukis also illustrated a representative collection of pottery and flint and stone tools from the hunebeds at full scale. He made beautiful water-coloured drawings of 27 TRB* pots in the Assen and Leiden museums, but also of 105 TRB* sherds, the first pictures of TRB* sherds in the Netherlands (Lukis 1879). Dryden drew an extra set of his plans and elevations for the Drenthe Museum of Antiquities at Gratama's request.[44] Unfortunately costs prevented publication.

Despite Fergusson's (1872) dating of the Drenthe hunebeds in the period ranging 'from the Christian era down to the time when the people of this country were converted to Christianity' (not unlike Gratama's ideas), the Stone Age date of what was in the 20th century to be called the Funnel Beaker or TRB culture, its types of pottery and megalithic tombs and their distribution became generally accepted as known facts before 1900.

No megalith research worth mentioning took place until 1912.[45] Unsystematic digging in the chamber fills by robbers went on until the early 1980s,[46] and hardly anything that was recovered reached the museums. "*It is my opinion that all hunebeds have been explored*" wrote the doctor and amateur archaeologist Douwe Lubach (1815-1902) as early as 1877 (Lubach 1877, 166). Fortunately this was not entirely true, and from 1912 onward the first systematic – though still much too hastily executed – excavations of Dutch hunebed chambers and sites of razed tombs were undertaken and published by Holwerda (1913a; 1913b; 1914) and van Giffen (1919; 1925-27; 1927; 1943). Only then were the first vertical sections through Dutch hunebeds drawn. Apart from Lukis's drawings, which were hidden in a London archive, the various forms and fashions of the astoundingly numerous pottery emerged now from the hunebed chambers.

EPILOGUE

Andrew Sherratt (1996) has discerned a dialectic between 'Enlightenment' and 'Romanticism' in the modes of European cultural and intellectual history and applied it to the history of archaeological thought. These two attitudes

---

[44] Four copies of Dryden's plans and elevations were made: they are kept in London (Society of Antiquaries, Burlington House), Assen (Drenthe Archives), Oxford (Dryden's bequest in the Ashmolean Museum) and in the Guernsey Museum (Lukis's bequest, pers. comm. H. Sebire, curator). Lukis's comments about and watercolours of hunebed pottery and flints as 'laid before the Society' together with Dryden's drawings in 1878 (Lukis 1879) are in Burlington House. His original notes are in the Guernsey Museum and the collected artefacts are in the British Museum.

[45] In 1904-10, W.J. de Wilde, an amateur archaeologist, copied Dryden's hunebed plans and checked them, made plans of the other hunebeds, described and photographed each one, and studied the TRB* pottery at the Assen museum. He knew Danish publications, stressed the importance of modern hunebed research and argued that, following the Danish example, an Inspector of the Hunebeds should be appointed. Holwerda would fulfil the first request in 1912 and van Giffen would fulfil both from 1918 onward. Unfortunately, most of de Wilde's papers are lost (Bakker 2004, 144-47).

[46] In 1983-85 a pavement of perforated concrete blocks was laid 15 cm deep on top of the not yet systematically excavated chamber fills of our hunebeds (Bakker 1992, 7, fig. 4).

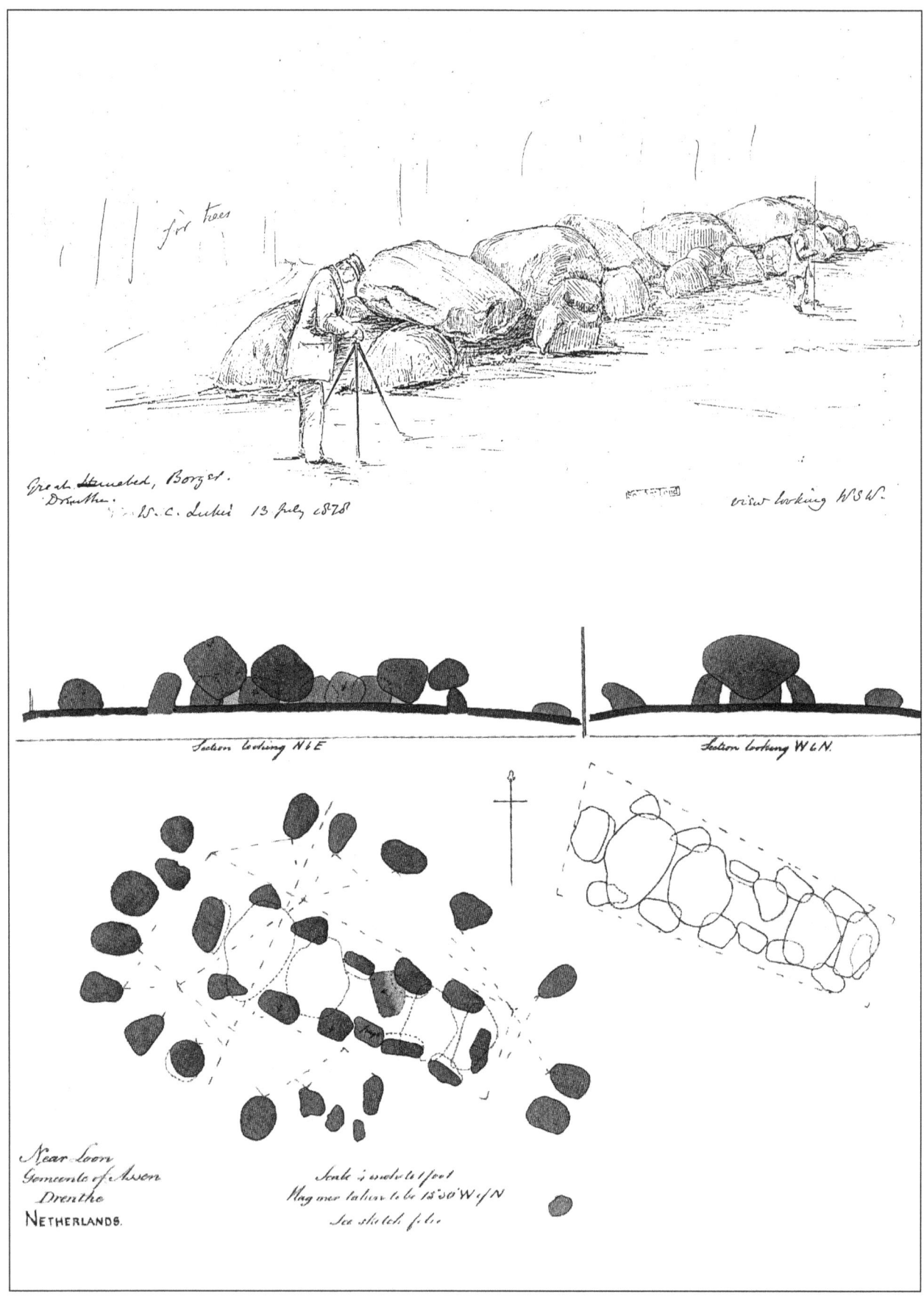

Fig. 2.5. a) H. Dryden is surveying the Great Hunebed D27 at Borger, 13 July 1878 (seen from the north). Pencil drawing by W.C. Lukis aided by a camera lucida (Society of Antiquaries, London); b) plan of hunebed D15-Loon by H. Dryden, ink and watercolour (Drenthe Archives, Assen)

reflect an alternation of 'action' and 'reaction', but rarely does the one become completely silenced by the other. As 'reconciliation' Sherratt noted that both movements could be united within the work of the same author. Undeniably there has also been a geographic or cultural bipolarity between the developments in Germany and France. In addition, T. Darvill (2006, Table A) placed an 'Age of myth and legend' before 'Reformation' as the earliest stage of the Romantic mode in this scheme, when he subdivided the research history of Stonehenge accordingly.

At first sight it would seem rather easy to discern the same alternation within the megalithic research in Drenthe. The medieval word *hunebed* reflects the 'Age of myth and legend'; Schonhovius (1547) worked in the 'Humanist Renaissance tradition'; the Calvinist Picardt (1660) with his Nordic giants may be labelled under 'Reformation'. Smids (1694), Hofstede & Kymmell (1706), van Lier (1760), Petrus Camper (1761-1789), J. and P. Hofstede (1809) represented the 'Enlightenment' mode. On the other hand, Adriaan Camper (1808), Westendorp (1815, 1822), Janssen (1847-1869), Gratama (1868-1886) and Pleyte (1870-1883) belonged to the 'Romantic' mode, whereas their English colleagues Franks (1872), Lukis and Dryden (1878) simultaneously represented the enlightened / positivist attitude.

On closer examination it is evident that adherents of a new mode retained important elements of the old. Schonhovius worked in the humanist tradition of the Renaissance, but still took for granted the Devil's Cunt myth and the giants (in the guise of 'Hercules'), which derived from the 'Age of myth and legend'. Smids (1694) wrote the first excavation report of a hunebed and he also saw that the bones in it were of normally sized people, but in 1711 he returned to the giants' theory. Kymmell and Hofstede (1706) wrote a brief, straightforward excavation report, but consulted the Italian renaissance author Alessandro for their theory that part of the pottery had contained provisions for the interred. Van Lier (1760) discussed at length hunebed D13 and its contents, for which he used French archaeological and ethnographic studies, as well as classical sources about the age and the civilisation of the builders. This was also done by the 'romantic' researcher Westendorp, who paid much attention to the stages of development of the hunebed builders – typical of the 'Enlightment' mode. Adriaan Camper was a typical enlightenment empirical scientist like his father Petrus, but he took a 'romantic' interest in the ethnic identification of the hunebed builders (1808).

According to the Dutch-German education system, one would perhaps be inclined to divide the attitudes towards Dutch hunebeds between the languages and history (*alpha*) and the natural sciences (*beta*) research traditions, with sociology (*gamma*) as a more recent development. This division is roughly comparable to Sherratt's, but the Renaissance study of Roman and Greek sources would then be moved to the 'Romantic' mode, and the beauty of the antiphony in Andrew's scheme would be disturbed.[47]

In some ways the approach of hunebed researchers reflects their education: Schonhovius, Picardt, J. Hofstede (1706), Westendorp, Janssen and Pleyte were educated in theology as priests or pastors. R.A. Kymmell, P. Hofstede, J. Hofstede (1808) and Gratama studied law. Picardt, Smids, P. and A.G. Camper studied medicine. Titia Brongersma was one of the rare poetesses of her time, and Smids was a poet, playwright and historian.

However, the main obstacle in applying Sherratt's scheme to the history of Dutch hunebed research, as Darvill did to that of Stonehenge, is that there was an ample choice of clear exponents of both attitudes among the Stonehenge studies, whereas the Dutch sample of hunebed studies is rather slim and several authors displayed no distinct approach or theory. Apart from Picardt, many Dutch authors seem more often followers than innovators of theories about hunebeds. Westendorp's work on West European megalithic tombs (1815, 1822), the legal protection of Drenthe hunebeds in 1734, and their acquisition by State and Province in 1868-80, was almost unique at the time.

References

ARENTZEN, W. (2005) *Janssiana I: De verzameling L.J.F. Janssen*. Utrecht: W. Arentzen, 165 p.

ARENTZEN, W. (2006) *Janssiana II: L.J.F. Janssen en de Hunen*. Utrecht: W. Arentzen, 266 p.

ARENTZEN, W. (2007) *Janssiana III: L.J.F. Janssen en het Gooi*. Utrecht: W. Arentzen.

BAKKER, J.A. (1978) Nordwestdeutsche Megalithgräber in niederländischen Berichten des 17. bis 19. Jahrhundert. *Die Kunde* N.F. 28-9, 1977-8 [1979], p. 21-31, pls. 1-2.

BAKKER, J.A. (1979a) *The TRB West Group. Studies in the chronology and geography of the makers of hunebeds and Tiefstich pottery*, Amsterdam: Universiteit van Amsterdam, Subfaculteit Pre- en Protohistorie, 238 p.

BAKKER, J.A. (1979b) Protection, acquisition, restoration and maintenance of the Dutch hunebeds since 1734: an active and often exemplary policy in Drenthe (I). *Berichten van de Rijksdienst voor het Oudheidkundig Bodemonderzoek* 29, p. 143-88.

---

[47] Moreover, it is not true that Humanism introduced 'modern, rational' approaches to Late Medieval historiography in western Europe between 1450 and 1550 (as has long been supposed). It added data from classical sources such as Tacitus, but usually retained the old myths and added new ones about the origin of tribes and towns, and humanist historiography had distinct local patriotic traits. The 'Batavian myth', which located the Insula Batavorum and the Batavians of the Roman sources in Holland and Utrecht and not in the Betuwe in Gelderland, is an example. (Ebels-Hoving 1987, 234ff.; Tilmans 1987).

BAKKER, J.A. (1979c) July 1878: Lukis and Dryden in Drente. *The Antiquaries Journal*, 59:1, p. 9-18, pl. I-VI.

BAKKER, J.A. (1984) De opgraving in het Grote Hunebed te Borger door Titia Brongersma op 11 juni 1685. *Nieuwe Drentse Volksalmanak* 1984, p. 103-16.

BAKKER, J.A. (1989) Petrus en Adriaan Camper en de hunebedden. In Schuller Tot Peursum-Meijer, J.; Koops, W.H.R., eds., (1989): – *Petrus Camper (1722-1789) onderzoeker van nature*. Groningen: Universiteits museum, p. 189-98.

BAKKER, J.A. (1990) Views on the Stone Age, 1848-1931: the impact of the 1853 Hilversum finds on Dutch prehistoric archaeology. *Berichten van de Rijksdienst voor het Oudheidkundig Bodemonderzoek* 40, p. 73-99.

BAKKER, J.A. (1992) *The Dutch hunebedden, megalithic tombs of the Funnel Beaker Culture*. Ann Arbor, Michigan: International Monographs in Prehistory. Archaeological Series 2.

BAKKER, J.A. (1999) The Dutch megalithic tombs, with a glance at those of North-West Germany. In Beinhauer, K.W.; Cooney, G.; Guksch, C.E.; Kus, S.. eds., (1999): *Studien zur Megalithik. Forschungsstand und ethnoarchäologische Perspektiven / The Megalithic phenomenon. Recent research and ethnoarchaeological approaches*, Mannheim-Weissbach: Beier & Beran, p. 145-62.

BAKKER, J.A. (2002) Hunebed de Duvelskut bij Rolde. *Nieuwe Drentse Volksalmanak* 119, p. 62-94.

BAKKER, J.A. (2004) *Kanttekeningen bij mijn publicaties en enige andere zaken*, Baarn: J.A. Bakker, 240 p.

BAKKER, J.A. (2005) De Steen en het rechthuis te Lage Vuursche. *Tussen Vecht en Eem*: Bussum, 23, p. 221-31.

BAKKER, J.A. (in press) Hunebedden and *Hünengräber*. The construction of megalithic tombs west of the River Elbe. *Papers XV session Union Internationale des Sciences Pré- et Protohistoriques, Lissabon, September 2006*.

BAKKER, J.A. (in preparation) *Hunebed D26 in het Drouwenerveld, verslag van de onderzoekingen*.

CAMPER, P. (1768, 1769, 1781) *De hunnen bedden van Drenthe Getekend door P. Camper* [1768, 1769, 1781]. Manuscript query with notes by P. and A.G. Camper, from 1768 to 1811. University Library Amsterdam, MS II G 53.

COHAUSEN, J.H. (1714) Ossilegium Historico-Physicum [...]. In Nunningh (1714).

DANIEL, G. (1981) *A Short History of Archaeology*. London: Thames and Hudson.

DARVILL, T. (2006) *Stonehenge. The biography of a landscape*. Stroud: Tempus.

DE BRUIJN, J.G. (1977): – *Inventaris van de prijsvragen uitgeschreven door de Hollandsche Maatschappij der Wetenschappen 1753-1917*. Haarlem: Hollandsche Maatschappij der Wetenschappen / Groningen: H.D. Tjeenk Willink, 551 p.

DEHN, T.; HANSEN, S.I. (2006) Birch bark in Danish passage graves. *Journal of Danish Archaeology* 14, p.23-44.

DE RHOER, J. (1770) *Oratio de fructu qui ex antiquitatis patriae studio in omne doctrinarum genus redit*. Groningen.

DE RHOER, J. (1774-1790) *Gesteldheid en geschiedenis van Drente*. Manuscript in Drenthe Archives, Assen, Coll. Gratama 233.

DE RHOER, J. (n.d.) Eene plaatselyke beschryving van Westerwoldingerland. *Verhandelingen Pro Excolendo* IV (2), 1ff.

EBELS-HOVING, B. (1987) Nederlandse geschiedschrijving 1350-1530. Een poging tot karakterisering. In Ebels-Hoving, B.; Santing, C.G; Tilmans, C.P.H.M., eds., (1987): – *Genoechlicke ende lustighe historiën. Laatmiddeleeuwse geschiedschrijving in Nederland*. Hilversum: Verloren, p. 216-242.

FERGUSSON, J. (1872) *Rude Stone Monuments in All Countires: Their Age and Uses*. London: Murray.

FRANKS, A.W. (1872) The megalithic monuments of the Netherlands and the means taken by the government of that country for their preservation. *Proceedings of the Society of Antiquaries of London*, 2nd series v (1870-1873), February 8, 1872, p. 258-67.

FRANKS, A.W. (1873): – [Translation of the report of the King's Commissioner in Drenthe, L.J.G. Gregory, in *Provinciale Drentsche en Asser Courant*, first translated into French by L. Oldenhuis Gratama]. *Proceedings of the Society of Antiquaries of London*, 2nd series v (1870-1873), March 20, 1873, 475ff.

FUCHS, J.M.; SIMONS, W.J. (1977) *Het zal je maar gezegd wezen. Buitenlanders over Nederland*. Den Haag: Kruseman.

GRATAMA, L. OLDENHUIS (1868) *Open brief aan het Collegie van Gedeputeerde Staten van Drenthe over de zorg voor en het onderhoud der hunnebedden, naar aanleiding der beraadslagingen over dat onderwerp in de vergadering van Provinciale Staten van Drenthe van November 1867*. Assen: van Gorcum en comp., 58 p.

GRATAMA, L. OLDENHUIS (1886) *De hunnebedden in Drenthe en aanverwante onderwerpen*. Assen.

GRIMM, J. (1844) *Deutsche Mythologie*, 2nd ed. (reprint Basel, 1953).

[GRIMM, W.K] (1824) [anonymous review of Westendorp 1822]. *Göttingsche gelehrte Anzeigen unter der Aufsicht der Königl. Gesellschaft der Wissenschaften*, 70.-71. Stück, p. 689-711.

GUMMEL, H. (1938) *Forschungsgeschichte in Deutschland*. Berlin: Walter de Gruyter & Co.

HERM, G. (1975) *Die Kelten*. Düsseldorf-Vienna. (Dutch transl. Baarn, 1992).

HERODOTUS (1974) *Herodotos Historiën, vertaling Dr. Onno Damsté*. Bussum: Fibula-van Dishoeck, 3rd ed.

HOLWERDA, J.H. (1913a) Opgraving van twee hunnebedden te Drouwen, *Oudheidkundige Mededeelingen uit 's Rijksmuseum van Oudheden te Leiden* 7, p. 29-50.

HOLWERDA, J.H. (1913b) Zwei Riesenstuben bei Drouwen (Prov. Drente) in Holland, *Prähistorische Zeitschrift* 5, p. 435-448.

HOLWERDA, J.H. (1914) Das grosse Steingrab bei Emmen (Prov. Drente), *Prähistorische Zeitschrift* 6, p. 57-67.

JACOB-FRIESEN, K.H.(1954) Johan Picardt, der erste Urgeschichtsforscher Niedersachsens. *Nachrichten aus Niedersachsens Urgeschichte* 23.

JANSSEN, L.J.F. (1848) *Drenthsche Oudheden*, Utrecht: Kemink & Zoon, 193 p.

JANSSEN, L.J.F. (1853a) Over de beschaving der allervroegste bewoners van ons vaderland afgeleid uit gevonden overblijfselen (eene archaeologische voorlezing). *Oudheidkundige Verhandelingen en Mededeelingen van Dr. L.J.F. Janssen* (I). Arnhem: I.A. Nijhoff en zoon, p. 1-26.

JANSSEN, L.J.F. (1853b) Hilversumsche oudheden, *Oudheidkundige Verhandelingen en Mededeelingen van Dr. L.J.F. Janssen* (I). Arnhem: I.A. Nijhoff en zoon, p. 137-60.

JUNIUS, H. (1588) *Batavia*. Leiden.

KAHLKE, H.D. (1981) *Das Eiszeitalter*. Leipzig-Jena-Berlin: Urania Verlag, 192 p.

KALB, P.H. (1990) Neue Ergebnisse zur Megalithkultur auf der Iberischen Halbinsel. *Nachrichten aus Niedersachsens Urgeschichte*, 49, p. 73-93.

KEMPIUS, C. (1580) *De origine, situ, qualitate et quantitate Frisiae, et rebus a Frisiis olim praeclare gestis, libri tres*. Cologne.

KLEMM, G.F. (1836) *Handbuch der germanischen Altertumskunde*. Dresden.

KLINDT-JENSEN, O. (1975) *A History of Scandinavian Archaeology*. London: Thames and Hudson.

KLOMPMAKER, II.; NIJKEUTER, H.; TISSING, J. (1996) *Poëzie van hunebedden. Een cultuurtoeristische benadering*. Zuidwolde: Het Drentse Boek, 106 p.

LIEBERS, C. (1986) *Neolithische Megalithgräber in Volksleben und Volksglauben. Untersuchung historischer Quellen zur Volksüberlieferung, zum Denkmalschutz und zur Fremdenverkehrswerbung*. Frankfurt am Main–Bern–New York: Peter Lang, 1986, 207 p.

LUGT, F. (1915) *Wandelingen met Rembrandt in en om Amsterdam*. Amsterdam: P.N. van Kampen & zoon.

LUKIS, W.C. (1879) Report on the hunebedden of Drenthe, Netherlands. *Proceedings of the Society of Antiquaries of London*, 2nd series viii (1879-1881), p. 47-55.

NIJKEUTER, H. (2001) *De "pen gewijd aan Drenthe's dierbren grond". Literaire bedrijvigheid in de Olde Lantschap, 1816-1956*. Doctoral thesis Groningen University.

NIJKEUTER, H. (2005) Titia Brongersma, 'de tiende der muzen' geïnspireerd door de Olde Lantschap. In Klompmaker, H. and Nijkeuter, H. *Dichter bij het hunebed*. Zuidwolde: Het Drentse boek, p. 27-41.

NUNNINGH, J.H.[48] (1713) *Sepulcretum Westphalico-Mimigardico Gentile [...]*. Coesfeld: B. Haustatt. The 2nd ed. (Frankfurt and Leipzig: M.A. Fuhrman, 1714) also contains Cohausen (1714). See also Hüsing's translation (1855).

OLEARIUS, J.C. (1701) *Museum in museo [...]*. Jena.

PICARDT, J. (1660) *Korte beschryvinge van eenige vergetene en verborgene Antiquiteten der Provintien en Landen gelegen tusschen de Nord-Zee, de Yssel, Emse en Lippe. Waer by gevoeght zijn Annales Drenthiae [...]. Mitsgaders eene korte Beschrijvinge der Stadt, des Casteels, en der Heerlickheyt Covorden*. Amsterdam: Gerrit van Goedesbergh, 302 p. (2nd ed. 1731, Groningen: Wed. J. Cost; 3rd ed. 1745, Groningen).

PLEYTE, W. (1877-1902) *Nederlandsche Oudheden van de Vroegste Tijden tot op Karel den Groote*, Leiden: E.J. Brill.

SCHELE VAN WELEVELT, S. (1589-1637) *Hausbuch oder Chronik 1589-1637*, manuscript: 1822 p., State archives Osnabrück and Overijssel archives Zwolle.

SHERRATT, A. (1996) 'Settlement patterns' or 'landscape studies'? Reconciling Reason and Romance. *Archaeological Dialogues* 3, p. 140-159.

SCHILSTRA, J.J. (1974) *In de ban van de dijk. De Westfriese Omringdijk*. Hoorn: West-Friesland (4th ed. 1982).

SCHNAPP, A. (1993) *The discovery of the past, the origins of archaeology*. London: British Museum Press, 384 p. (transl. from the French, Paris 1993).

SCHULZE, W. (1959) Jacobus Tollius und die Grosssteingräber bei Magdeburg. Ein Beitrag zur Geschichte der Vorgeschichtsforschung. *Jahresschrift für mitteldeutsche Vorgeschichte* 43, p. 121-126, pl. 4.

SEGER, H. (1930) Die Anfänge des Dreiperioden-Systems. In *Schumacher Festschrift*, Mainz, p. 3-7.

SIPPEL, K. (1980) Die Kenntnis vorgeschichtlicher Hügelgräber im Mittelalter. *Germania* 58, p. 137-146.

SMIDS, L. (1694) *Poësye*. Amsterdam.

SMIDS, L. (1711) *Schatkamer der Nederlandsse Oudheden; of Woordenboek, behelsende Nederlands

---

[48] Nunningh's signature on the title page of Hamconius' *Frisia* (1609) (internet, uni.muenster) shows that he wrote his name without an umlaut: "J.H. Nunningh / Dr. Schol. Vred[..]". Hüsing's spelling (1855) 'Nünningh' is incorrect.

Steden en Dorpen, Kastelen, Sloten en Heeren Huysen, Oude Volkeren, Rivieren, Vermaarde Luyden in Staat en Oorlog, Oudheden, Gewoontens en Lands wysen. Amsterdam: P. de Coup, 17 + 402 + 26 p.

SPROCKHOFF, E. (1966, 1967, 1975) *Atlas der Megalithgräber Deutschlands, Teil 1: Schleswig-Holstein* (1966); *Teil 2: Mecklenburg-Brandenburg-Pommern* (1967); *Teil 3: Niedersachsen-Westfalen, aus dem Nachlass herausgegeben von G. Körner* (1975) Bonn: R. Habelt (each consisting of a Textvol. and an atlas).

STEMMERMANN, P.H. (1934) *Die Anfänge der deutschen Vorgeschichtsforschung: Deutschlands Bodenaltertümer in der Anschauung des 16. und 17. Jahrhunderts*. Quakenbrück.

STRAAT, P.; VAN DER DEURE, P. (1733) *Ontwerp tot een minst kostbaare, zeekerste en schielykste herstelling van de zorgelyke toestand der Westfriesche zeedyken; zonder dat het voortknagend Zeegewormte daar aan eenige hindernisse kan veroorsaken.*, Amsterdam (2nd ed. 1735).

TILMANS, K. (1987) Cornelius Aurelius en het ontstaan van de Bataafse mythe in de Hollandse geschiedschrijving (tot 1517). In Ebels-Hoving, B.; Santing, C.G.

TILMANS, C.P.H.M., eds., (1987) *Genoechlicke ende lustighe historiën. Laatmiddeleeuwse geschiedschrijving in Nederland*. Hilversum: Verloren, p. 191-213.

[TONKENS, J., in co-operation with J. DE RHOER] (1795) *Inleiding. Tegenwoordige Staat van het Landschap Drenthe*. Amsterdam etc: J. de Groot etc., 120 p. (written before Tonkens's death in 1790, it appeared as a sequel to Van Lier (1790); the numbered notes are van Lier's).

VAN GIFFEN, A.E. (1919) Mededeeling omtrent onderzoek en restauratie van het groote hunebed te Havelte, *Nieuwe Drentsche Volksalmanak* 37, p. 109-139.

VAN GIFFEN, A.E. (1925-1927) *De hunebedden in Nederland*. Utrecht: A. Oosthoek. vol. I, 244 p.; vol. II, 580 p.; atlas, 3 p., 154 pl.

VAN GIFFEN, A.E. (1927) *The hunebeds in the Netherlands*. Utrecht: A. Oosthoek (transl. of Van Giffen (1925), vol. I, and Atlas.

VAN GIFFEN, A.E. (1943) Het Ndl. Hunebed (DXXVIII) te Buinen, Gem. Borger), een bijdrage tot de absolute chronologie der Nederlandsche hunebedden, *Nieuwe Drentsche Volksalmanak* 1943, p. 115-136.

VAN GINKEL, E.; JAGER, S.; VAN DER SANDEN, W. (1999) *Hunebedden, monumenten van een steentijdcultuur*. Abcoude: Uniepers.

VAN LIER, J. (1760) *Oudheidkundige Brieven, bevattende eene verhandeling over de manier van Begraven, en over de Lykbusschen, Wapenen, Veld- en Eertekens, der Oude Germanen, en in het byzonder de beschryving van eenen alouden Steenen Grafkelder, met de daarin gevondene Lykbusschen, Donderkeilen en Donderbylen, enz. By het Boerschap Eext, in het Landschap Drenthe, ontdekt, in welke beschryvinge zekere Brief, over byzondere Nederlandsche Oudheden, zo opgehelderd als wederlegd word. Door Mr. Joannes van Lier, Oud Gedeputeerde Staate, thans Ontfanger Generaal en Medelid van den Loffelyken Etstoel des Landschaps Drenthe. Met noodige afbeeldingen opgehelderd. Uitgegeeven en met Voorreden en Aantekeningen vermeerderd door A. Vosmaer*. The Hague: Pieter van Thol, 206 p., Pl. I-V.

[VAN LIER, J. in co-operation with his sons J.H.P. and F.A. VAN LIER] (1792) *Tegenwoordige Staat van het Landschap Drenthe, Eerste en Tweede stuk*. Amsterdam etc.: J. de Groot etc., xvi + 436 + 16 p. (published under the name of J.H.P. Van Lier; the volume by Tonkens (1795) was published as a sequel).

VERDAM, J. (1911) *Middelnederlandsch handwoordenboek*. The Hague: M. Nijhoff, 700 p.

VON ESTORFF, G.O.C. (1846) *Heidnische Alterthümer der Gegend von Uelzen im ehemaligen Bardengaue*, Hannover.

WEDEL, G.W.U. (1812) *Abhandlung über den Ursprung der alten Begräbniss-denkmäler im Departement Drenthe, zur Beantwortung der von der Kayserlichen Societaet der Wissenschaften zu Haarlem für den 1sten November 1812 aufgegebenen Preisfrage* (manuscript, HMW archives in Haarlem Archives), 81 p.

[WESTENDORP, N. (1812)] *Verhandeling over de Hunebedden. Ter beantwoording van de vrage, door de Maatschappy der Wetenschappen te Haarlem uitgeschreven, van inhoud: vrage: Welke Volkeren hebben de zoogenoemde hunebedden gesticht? In welke tyden kan men onderstellen, dat zy deze oorden hebben bewoond?* Anonymous ms., 152 p., under motto "A tous les coeurs bien nés, que la patrie est chère". The author's name and the date of Dec. 25, 1812 in a closed envelope carrying the motto. With 'Bijvoegsels' (Additions), 24 p. with a 2 p. letter, from early in 1813. Unpublished. HMW archives in Haarlem Archives.

WESTENDORP, N. (1815) Verhandeling ter beantwoording der vrage: Welke volkeren hebben de zoogenoemde hunebedden gesticht. In welke tijden kan men onderstellen, dat zij deze oorden hebben bewoond? *Letter- en Oudheidkundige Verhandelingen van de Hollandsche Maatschappij der Wetenschappen te Haarlem* I, 1815, p. 233-377.

WESTENDORP, N. (1822) *Verhandeling ter beantwoording der vrage: Welke volkeren hebben de zoogenoemde hunebedden gesticht. In welke tijden kan men onderstellen, dat zij deze oorden hebben bewoond?* Groningen: J. Oomkens: xvi + 328 + 51 p. (2nd, revised and enlarged edition, monograph).

WESTENDORP, N., ed. (1819-1823) *Antiquiteiten, een oudheidkundig tijdschrift, bezorgd door Nicolaus Westendorp*. Groningen: J. Oomkens. (part 2, 1823, was co-edited by C.J.C. Reuvens).

JEAN-MARIE BACHELOT DE LA PYLAIE (1786-1856) THE JOURNEY OF AN ARCHEOLOGIST AMONG THE ANTIQUARIES IN BRITTANY IN THE SECOND HALF OF THE XIXTH CENTURY

Serge CASSEN

CNRS (Unité Mixte de Recherche 6566), Laboratoire de Préhistoire et Protohistoire de l'Ouest de la France, Université de Nantes, BP 81227, 44312 NANTES cedex 3 (FRANCE), serge.cassen@univ-nantes.fr

Cyrille CHAIGNEAU

Laboratoire de Préhistoire et Protohistoire de l'Ouest de la France, Université de Nantes, BP 81227, 44312 NANTES cedex 3 (FRANCE), cyrille.chaigneau@univ-nantes.fr

English translation by Caroline Tonnerre

Abstract: Jean-Marie de la Pylaie was born in 1786 in Fougères at the gates of Brittany. His archeological works are little known, and completely underestimated. For 40 years he traveled Brittany relentlessly, and he developed a scientific process based on drawing the monuments and adding detailed comments. His method of work was very innovative for its time, and was directly inspired by the Société des Observateurs de l'Homme created during the French Revolution. He also wrote one of the first worthy descriptions of the Carnac and Locmariaquer monuments, which he visited from 1824 onward after many others. The recent rediscovery of his synoptic charts and other manuscripts show the particular and innovative processes of this researcher. In 2006, 150 years after Bachelot died, they restore to favour works of the first rank from an archaeologist in the time of antiquaries.
Key words: Megalithism, Carnac, monument classification, epistemology

Résumé: Jean-Marie de la Pylaie, né en 1786 à Fougères, demeure un inconnu parmi ces pionniers de l'archéologie armoricaine et française, alors que son travail, durant 40 ans, n'aura de cesse d'être fondé sur des descriptions rigoureuses et des dessins d'accompagnement fidèles. Ses méthodes sont inspirées par la Société des Observateurs de l'Homme créée au lendemain de la Révolution de 1789. Il est un des premiers à fournir une description valable des monuments du secteur Carnac-Locmariaquer. La récente découverte de ses manuscrits et tableaux synoptiques prouve les aspects innovants de sa recherche, en avance sur son temps. En 2006, 150 après la mort de Bachelot ces documents réhabilitent enfin la mémoire d'un archéologue au temps des antiquaires.
Mots clés: Mégalithisme, Carnac, classification des monuments, épistémologie

Jean-Marie de la Pylaie was born on 25th May, 1786 in Fougères at the gates of Brittany. He was first and foremost an extraordinarily curious and broad-minded botanist. He studied in Laval, then became the student of Georges Cuvier and de Blainville – among others – at the Musée National d'Histoire Naturelle in Paris (National Natural History Museum). He was a great traveler, mainly in France and in America, but also went to Newfoundland in 1816 and Saint-Pierre-et-Miquelon in 1820 at his own expense.

He became then the first known naturalist to gather a collection of local species. He dedicated a huge part of his naturalist activities to the systematic exploration of the Breton Islands (Belle-Ile, Sein, Houat, Hoëdic, Noirmoutier, Ile-Dieu). He was the instigator of the study of North American algae, a forerunner in the studies of lichens, mosses and Atlantic fish species. He also wrote one of the first treatises in conchyliology. Bachelot left us considerable naturalist works, whose lead, originality and value have been shown in recent studies.

His archeological works are a lot less known, and completely underestimated. He became an archaeologist because it was his vocation and, in the spirit of the Académie Celtique (Celtic Academy), he devoted himself to the study of prehistory although it was only just beginning to be studied. Prehistory was then considered, within a short biblical chronology, in the "celtophile" approach of the druidical monuments. 31 published articles as well as 23 unpublished manuscripts demonstrate his activities in the subject.

For 40 years he traveled Brittany relentlessly, and developed a scientific process based on drawing the monuments and adding detailed comments. His method of work was very innovative for its time, and directly inspired by the Société des Observateurs de l'Homme (Society of Observers of Mankind) created during the French Revolution. Bachelot explained this work method several times in various manuscripts and published articles:

> "These monuments so often visited, studied, explained still remain a mystery to archaeologists! Each of them has seen and described them in his/her own way, and too often with prejudice, so that the monuments were known neither the way they globally exist, nor in the correlation of the parts. (...) The reason why I have not wanted to know anything about my peers' works is because I was keen to stay away from their opinions: first of all I wanted to remain myself. (...) As far as I am concerned I am far from considering myself

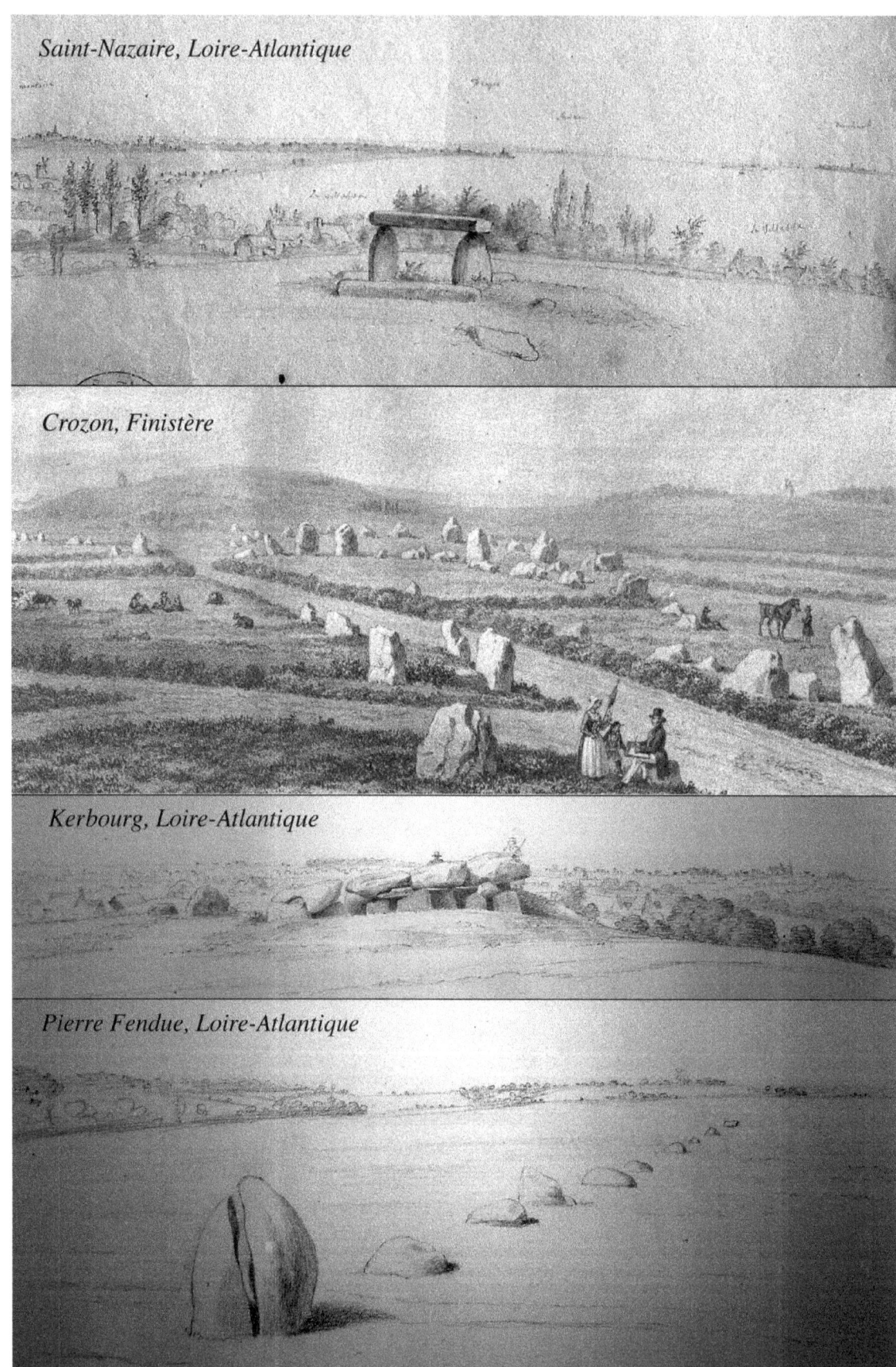

Fig. 3.1. Bachelot's drawings of several megalithic sites (Saint-Nazaire passage grave with form of its cairn – now inside the city; Crozon alignment – destroyed; Kerbourg passage grave with the form of the cairn; Pierre Fendue alignment in the Brière marshland – destroyed). Institut de France, (Archives de l'Académie des inscriptions et belles-lettres, dossier 3 H 162 à 165 – 1836; Bachelot 1850)

infallible, but in order to prevent any prejudice or the effects of imagination or sometimes bad memory, I observe and describe every object on the spot, I draw it and I even make a plan, depending on how important the object is. Then I go to libraries for complementary work. This is the method I compel myself to, and I will always comply with it. Perhaps I will be verbose? But I believe that in many cases it is better to give a detailed description than to draw a portrait of a person with only a few facial features."

Then he continued:

"Since the different works on one object can only be appreciated when compared to one another, I have judged that comparison was giving me the best opportunity to show how poor the descriptions of the time were."

Such diplomatic phrasing so that he could better criticise those works he considered as scientifically unworthy!

Bachelot applied this method of work to every location he visited. He created the Cojou megalithic complex in Saint Just and in the Lande du Moulin de Langon (Ille-et-Vilaine), as well as the monuments in the Brière swamps in the Loire-Atlantique, the now destroyed large systems on the Crozon peninsula and in Menez Hom in Finistère. He also wrote one of the first worthy descriptions of the Carnac and Locmariaquer monuments, which he visited from 1824 onward after many others.

Then, in 1825, as a recently affiliated member of the Société des Antiquaires de France (Society of French Antiquaries), he presented the results of his work, but his scientific demands worried and upset some eminent members of the scholarly assembly. The session reports reveal the keen competition among the antiquaries when it came to these famous sites.

Chevalier de Fréminville and Sébastien Jorand in particular stood in Bachelot's way. In the end, he would not have the right to publish his works in antiquarian publications. The article Bachelot wrote on Carnac was integrated in 1840 into the researches of the Institut Historique (Historical Institute). This limited its dissemination in the archeological field since it was not mentioned in any bibliography about megalithism in Morbihan. Yet Bachelot was not discouraged by the antiquaries' distrust, and he used every opportunity to broadcast his works. He was a key figure at the Congrès Scientifique de Poitiers (Poitiers Scientific Congress) organized by Arcisse de Caumont in 1834. There he showed among others a Carnac plan (which has been lost) and gave a long description of the Carnac Alignments.

Bachelot first objected to the various theories that had been suggested and accepted about the purpose of the Carnac monuments, then presented his own: Carnac had been built to worship the stars, and the sun and the moon played a role in specific sites (Saint-Michel-Kerkado). He presented this astronomic system many times, doubtless one of the first of its kind.

In 1831 he described the megalithic monuments at the mouth of the Loire and discovered an architecture type he had never seen before (the transept type). He wrote:

"Since this layout is still new to me, I believe I can conclude without going too far that the religious system in this part of Armorica was separated from that in the rest of the country. I have traveled Brittany left, right and center, and saw more dolmens, menhirs and cromlechs than anybody else. I draw them at once, and may I one day be happy enough to deduce a kind of philosophical classification out of their shapes, their orientations, and the differences in the stone types they are made of."

He then worked relentlessly to build this classification, and in 1836 he published three *"Tableaux synoptiques présentant un essai sur la classification des monuments celtiques"* (Synoptic Charts Presenting an Attempt at Classification of Celtic Monuments) in the Journal de l'Institut Historique (Journal of the Historical Institute). The article, in which Bachelot suggested a taxonomic approach to the Armorican megalithism based on a catalogue of hundreds of monuments, oddly remained a dead letter and completely unknown in the antiquarian community. The Ille-et-Vilaine Department Archives have recently bought documents from another Fougères scholar, Théodore Danjou de la Garenne, which have enabled identification of the preliminary notes and complete version of these leading and unique works of French archaeology in the first half of the XIXth century.

There are a few keys to helping to understand these charts in a note entitled *"Observation sur l'Histoire de l'Architecture Religieuse dans la Bretagne Armoricaine et les Provinces Limitrophes"* (Observation on the History of Religious Architecture in Armorican Brittany and in the Border Provinces), presented on December 12th, 1835 at the 13th Congrès Historique Européen (European Historical Congress) in Paris, and published by the Institut Historique in 1836.

Bachelot had to deal with the complexity of Megalithic Architecture which he could understand thanks to the unique corpus he had been able to gather, so he proposed these *"three synoptic charts in which I have forced myself to classify our Celtic monuments as simply and as completely as I could"*. Thus Bachelot organized his corpus made of hundreds of documents into three main classes:

1. Monuments projecting from the ground – single stones or stones not superimposed (for menhirs); and monuments erected above the ground – stones superimposed in voluminous blocks (for dolmens)

2. Stones embedded in the ground so that only their tops are seen

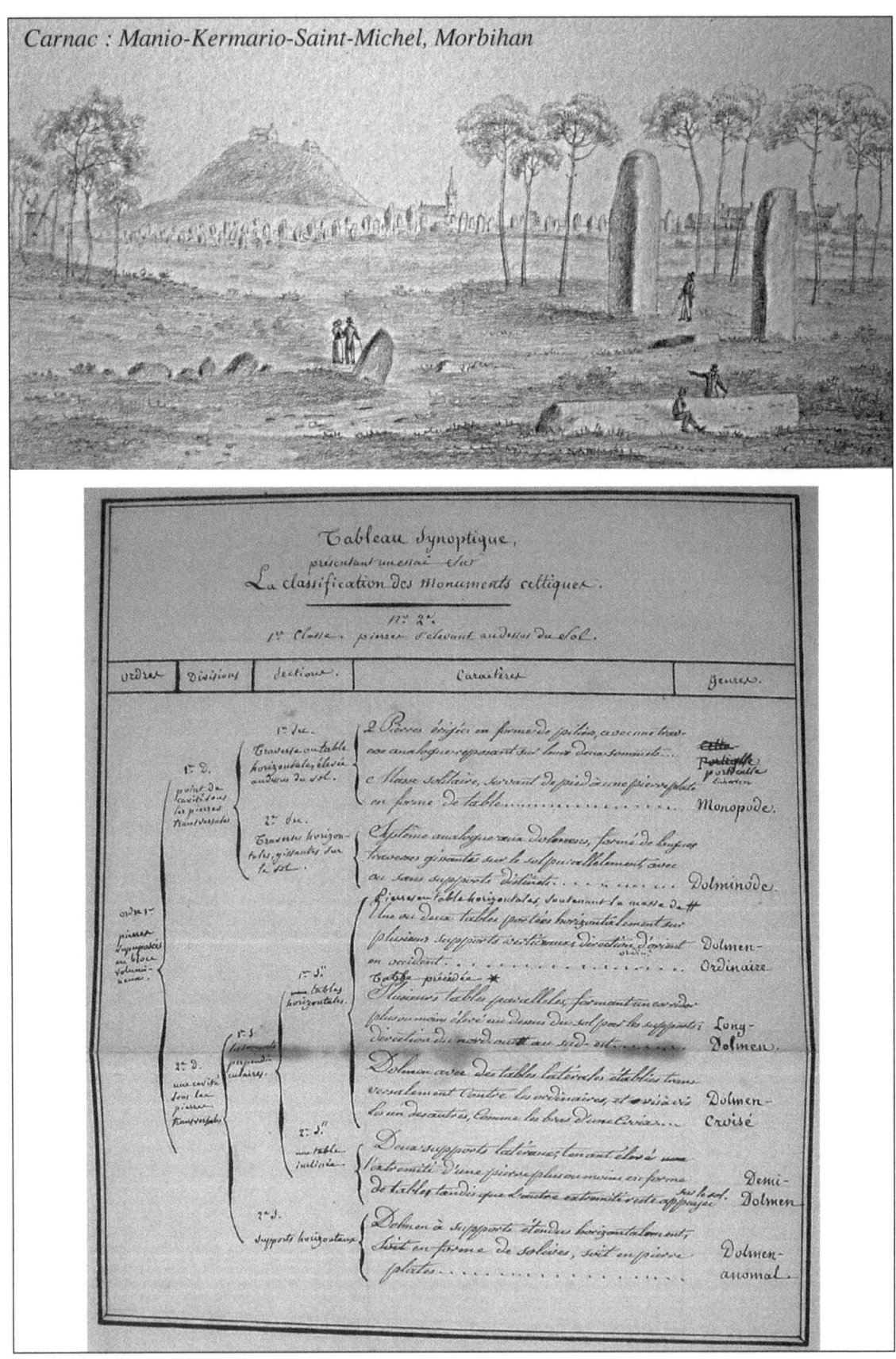

Fig. 3.2. Drawing by Bachelot of Carnac alignments: view from the Manio "giants" and "quadrilatère" remains in the direction of St-Michel tumulus (with a double edifice on the top); on the left Kermaux windmill and, in the centre, Kermario lines. Synoptic Chart presents an attempt at the classification of Celtic monuments (Institut de France, Archives de l'Académie des inscriptions et belles-lettres, dossier 3 H 162 à 165 – 1824; Archives départementales d'Ille-et-Vilaine, 1 J 598 – 1830-35)

3. Monuments made of conglomerate loose stones with various amounts of earth.

Then he used these three main classes to define 36 types of monument and created a complete scientific terminology, inspired – which is extremely important – by popular languages such as Breton or Brittany's Gallo. So "Toënti" describes the angled dolmens in Finistère, and "Belion" is the word used by peasants in the Land of Redon for the large quartz boulders scattered on the moor.

There is one essential thing in these works: Bachelot described each of the monuments as such, and never took the notion of ruin into account. Thus he placed the same kind of monuments (for instance passage graves) into different categories, depending on their state of ruin. Moreover, his naturalist education led him to study Breton geology. He wrote numerous things about this, and here is Bachelot as geologist who first noticed that the orthogneiss found in some of the Locmariaker monuments was not derived locally:

> "Speaking about Locmariaker, some parts of the monuments there, one of their tables or capstones is not made of the same material as the rest, and it also does not come from local areas either. So I believe I can consider it as the main part, the shrine's sacred stone, maybe the sacrifice table. As far as I know, nobody has ever noticed it, although it is extremely important."

Bachelot was a militant for institutional protection of this heritage. Yet in 1828, despite his recommendations to Fougères sub-prefect Mr. Deslandes, the huge megalithic site in Mont-Bêleu wood was destroyed so that the stones could be used for the construction of the road to Laval. Bachelot was particularly shocked by this. Thus he said at the Congrès Scientifique de Poitiers in 1834:

> *"Despite their fame, the most remarkable granite boulders of the Carnac and Locmariaker monuments were scheduled to be used in the construction of the Breton canal locks. The monuments were only preserved because the magnificent stones were too far from the building site and difficult to carry there. All the dolmens and menhirs situated along the canal shores are gone."*

He repeatedly suggested protection measures to prevent the mass destructions that were occurring at that time, but his militancy had hardly any effect. He therefore sometimes talked directly to politicians; in 1843 he wrote a letter to the mayor of Lanvéoc on the Crozon peninsula:

> *"Dear Mr. Mayor,*
> *Since the monuments left by our ancestors the Gauls are disappearing a little more every day, and France is in danger of losing the last of its most ancient historical titles, it is my duty to remind Your Honour of all the dolmens, menhirs, peulvans, mounds or barrows made of earth or dry stones, as well as all the other stones linked to various traditions.*

> *Please remind your fellow citizens that these monuments have only been preserved until today because our ancestors worshipped them either as religious objects, or as testimonies of facts to be remembered by posterity, and also to honour famous men: please remind your citizens that these monuments have thus become national property.*

> *But above all, please remind all the people owning these monuments on their estates that they have to leave them untouched, wherever they are, for they have been there for centuries, so there is a moral duty to preserve them, whatever the landowners demand.*

> *Finally, the monuments are under the protection of the government, thus every alteration or damage caused to them will be as strongly punished as alterations or damage to churches, crosses, and public buildings of all kind: it will lead to prison and hard labour in the event of a second offence."*

Then again, we can read in the reports of the Congrès de la Classe d'Archéologie de l'Association Bretonne (Congress of Archaeology Classes of the Breton Association) which took place in Rennes in 1844:

> *"Mr. de la Pylaie gives a few details regarding his archeological expeditions. After having reported several recent vandalistic offences, the honorable member makes a proposal. This is that the congress should require the so-called druidic stones to be declared state property, and thus placed under the protection of criminal laws. Mr. de Blois understands the feeling that has inspired the author of the proposal, yet he does not believe, he says, that it can conform to the principles of property legislation. The assembly supports the latter opinion, and decides there is no ground for accepting Mr. de la Pylaie's proposal."*

Here again, Bachelot was certainly ahead of his time. But the recent re-discovery of the synoptic charts and other manuscripts shows the particular and innovative processes of this researcher. In 2006, 150 years after Bachelot died, they restore to favour works of the first rank from an archaeologist in the time of antiquaries.

Bachelot's Archaeological Publications

BACHELOT, J.M. 1814, *Précis géologique sur le bassin calcaire et tertiaire des environs de Dinan.*- S.l. n.d..- in-12°, 254 p.

BACHELOT, J.M. 1829c, "Notice sur la ville de Sainte-Suzanne [dans le Maine], sur les débris des fortifications vitrifiées de son ancien château et sur les dolmens situés dans son voisinage, par M. de la Pylaie, correspondant de la Société royale des antiquaires", dans: *Mémoires de la Société des antiquaires de France*, 1ère série, t. 8, 1826-1829 [1829].- p. 357-370.

BACHELOT, J.M. 1831?, *Recherches au Vieux-Poitiers et au bourg de Cenon en 1831*, par M. de la Pylaie.

BACHELOT, J.M. 1831a, "Fragment sur une chaussée romaine dans le département du Morbihan", extrait d'une lettre de M. de la Pylaie dans: *Mélanges d'archéologie précédés d'une notice historique sur la Société royale des antiquaires de France et du 5ᵉ rapport sur ses travaux*.- Paris, Séb. Bottin, 1831.- p. 218-220.

BACHELOT, J.M. 1831b, "Extrait d'une lettre de M. de la Pylaie; membre de la Société au même [M. Jomard], Langon, le 12 janvier 1831 [relation de son voyage le long de la Vilaine]", dans: *Bulletin de la Société de géographie*, t. 15, n° 95, mars 1831.- Paris, chez Arthus-Bertrand, libraire de la Société de géographie, 1831.- p. 143-144.

BACHELOT, J.M. 1831c, "Extrait d'une lettre de M. de la Pylaie; membre de la Société de géographie, à M. Jomard, Paimbœuf, le 17 août 1831 [sur les antiquités romaines des bords de la Loire]", dans: *Bulletin de la Société de géographie*, t. 16, n° 101, septembre 1831.- Paris, chez Arthus-Bertrand, libraire de la Société de géographie, 1831.- p. 140-143.

BACHELOT, J.M. 1832, "Lettre de M. de la Pilaye sur les antiquités de Noirmoutier, à M. Huette, membre de la Société académique et opticien à Nantes", dans: *Annales de la Société royale académique de Nantes et du département de la Loire-Inférieure*, 3ᵉᵐᵉ vol., 15ᵉᵐᵉ livraison, 1832.- p. 168-172.

BACHELOT, J.M. 1834a, [Diverses interventions], dans: *Congrès scientifique de France*, 2ᵉᵐᵉ session, tenue à Poitiers en septembre 1834.- p. 28, 30, 42, 48, 50, 68, 79, 83, 91, 98, 110, 160, 162, 169, 174, 183, 185, 187, 189, 190, 524-534, 583-588.

BACHELOT, J.M. 1834b, "Les monuments mégalithiques de l'île Dieu", dans: *Congrès scientifique de France*, 2ᵉᵐᵉ session, tenue à Poitiers en septembre 1834.- p. 183-187.

BACHELOT, J.M. 1834c, "Précis géologique sur le bassin de calcaire tertiaire des environs de Dinan, par M. de la Pylaie, membre de diverses académies et sociétés savantes", dans: *L'Annuaire dinannais*, 1834.- p. 205-254.

BACHELOT, J.M. 1835, "Animaux fossiles.- Note de M. DE LA PYLAIE sur des os de crocodiles et de tortue, trouvés aux environs de Sablé (Sarthe)", dans: *Compte-rendu hebdomadaires des séances de l'Académie des sciences*, 1835.- p. 438-439, séance du lundi 7 décembre 1835, présidence de M. Ch. Dupin.

BACHELOT, J.M. 1836a, *Recherches et découvertes archéologiques faites depuis Nantes jusqu'à l'embouchure de la Loire, par M. de la Pylaie*.- Nantes, imp. d'Hérault, 1836.- in-8°, 8 p.

BACHELOT, J.M. 1836b, "Notice sur l'ancienne église de Notre-Dame-Garde-Fortune et des Périls, aujourd'hui dite de Prisce, près Laval par [Bachelot] de la Pylaie", dans: *L'annuaire de la Mayenne*, 1836.

BACHELOT, J.M. 1836c, "13ᵉᵐᵉ séance. 12 décembre 1835. Observations sur l'histoire de l'architecture religieuse dans la Bretagne armoricaine et les provinces limitrophes, par M. de la Pylaie", dans: *Congrès historique européen, réuni à Paris au nom de l'Institut historique dans la salle Saint-Jean, à l'Hôtel-de-Ville – Discours et compte-rendu des Séances – Novembre-Décembre 1835*.- Paris, A. Leclaire et Cie libraires de l'Institut historique, 1836.- t. 2, p. 191-198.

BACHELOT, J.M. 1836d, "La Roche aux Fées, dépᵗ d'Ille-et-Vilaine, par M. de la Pylaie, associé correspondant", dans: *Mémoires de la Société des antiquaires de France*, 2ᵉᵐᵉ série, t. 12, 1834-1836 [1836], B.- p. 95-103.

BACHELOT, J.M. 1836-1837a, "Découvertes archéologiques faites dans l'Ouest de la France, depuis 1830 jusqu'à la fin de 1836", dans: *Journal de l'Institut historique*, 1ᵉʳᵉ série, 3ᵉᵐᵉ année, t. 5, 1836-1837.- in-8°, p. 246-257.

BACHELOT, J.M. 1836-1837b, "Tableaux synoptiques, présentant un essai sur la classification des monuments celtiques", dans: *Journal de l'Institut historique*, 1ᵉʳᵉ série, 3ᵉᵐᵉ année, t. 5, 1836-1837.- in-8°, p. 258-260.

BACHELOT, J.M. 1837, "Nouvelle découverte de quelques antiquités", dans: *Journal de l'Institut historique*, 1ᵉʳᵉ série, 4ᵉᵐᵉ année, t. 7, 1837.- in-8°, p. 13-18.

BACHELOT, J.M. 1838a, "La ville d'Avran, près de Fougères, département d'Ille-et-Vilaine, par M. de la Pylaie, associé correspondant", dans: *Mémoires de la Société des antiquaires de France*, 2ᵉᵐᵉ série, t. 14, 1838.- in-8°, p. 30-35.

BACHELOT, J.M. 1838b, "La chapelle de Saint-André au bourg de Domagné, arrondissement de Vitré, par M. de la Pylaie, associé correspondant [ancien temple romain]", dans: *Mémoires de la Société des antiquaires de France*, 2ᵉᵐᵉ série, t. 14, 1838.- p. 85-97.

BACHELOT, J.M. 1838c, [...], dans: *Journal l'Armée*, 6 mai 1838 [à propos des travaux de Bachelot sur le Mont Gannelon près de Compiègne].

BACHELOT, J.M. 1839-1840a, "Monuments de Carnac (département du Morbihan), nouvelle explication", dans: *Journal de l'Institut historique*, 6ᵉᵐᵉ année, t. 11, 1839-1840.- in-8°, p. 42-53.

BACHELOT, J.M. 1839-1840b, "Mémoires. Excursion archéologique à Jublains. Observations sur les Diablintes et l'étendue de leur territoire", dans: *Journal de l'Institut historique*, 6ᵉᵐᵉ année, t. 11, 1839-1840.- in-8°, p. 193-204.

BACHELOT, J.M. 1840, "Notice sur les atterrissements formés par l'Océan dans la baie de Bourg-Neuf et sur quelques parties de la côte du Poitou", dans: *Journal de l'Institut historique*, 7ᵉᵐᵉ année, t. 12, 1840.- p. 154-156.

BACHELOT, J.M. [1841], *Recherches archéologiques dans le département de l'Oise. 1ᵉʳ. Camp romain et camp gaulois sur le mont Gannelon.*- s.l., s.d., 12 p.

BACHELOT, J.M. 1842a, "Quelle fut la disposition des théâtres chez les grecs et chez les Romains et quelles différences existèrent entre ces édifices chez les deux peuples?", dans: *L'Investigateur. Journal de l'Institut historique.*- 9ème année, 2ème série, t. 2, 1942.- p. 45-.

BACHELOT, J.M. 1842b, "Détermination du lieu resté incertain où se donna la bataille de Charles Martel contre Abdérame, roi des Sarrasins, et qui est la seule qu'on doive appeler la bataille de Poitiers", dans: *L'Investigateur. Journal de l'Institut historique.*- 9ème année, 2ème série, t. 2, 1942.- p. 54-57, 2 notes infra.

BACHELOT, J.M. 1843, *Fragments archéologiques mêlés d'observations et de notices diverses*, par M. Le Bᵒⁿ de la Pylaie.- Morlaix, imp. de Vᵉʳ Guilmer, 1843.- in-8°, 23 p.

BACHELOT, J.M. 1844a, *Esquisse de l'excursion que je fis dans les arrondissements de Lannion, Perros-Guirec, Tréguier, Châtelaudren.*- 8 p.

BACHELOT, J.M. 1844b, "Recherches archéologiques sur Lohéac", dans: *Revue bretonne*, 2ème année, t. 3, février 1844.- Brest.- p. 71-84.

BACHELOT, J.M. 1845a, *Sommaire de mon voyage archéologique dans le département des Côtes-du-Nord en 1845*, publié en partie dans le *Publicateur de Côtes du Nord* en 1845 et dans l'*Armoricain*, n° du 31 juillet et du 14 août 1845.

BACHELOT, J.M. 1845b, "Résultats de mes études archéologiques faites depuis Nantes jusqu'à l'embouchure de la Loire et dans ses environs", dans: *Revue de l'Armorique et de l'Ouest*, année 1845.- p. 194 et suiv.

BACHELOT, J.M. [1847], *Recherches archéologiques dans la commune de Moelens [Moëlan] près de Quimperlé. Notice sur saint Melaine, patron de Moëlan.*- S.l., imp. E. Duverger, rue de Verneuil, s.d. [1847].-in-8°, 63 p., 24 cm.

BACHELOT, J.M. [1848]a, *Notice sur l'île de Sein*, par A.-J.-M. de la Pylaie.- Brest, imp. de C. Le Blois, [1848].- in-8°.

BACHELOT, J.M. 1848b, "Visite à l'ancienne fortification de Borghstadt, nommé depuis camp de Q. Cicéron, situé à l'occident du bourg d'Assche, auprès de Bruxelles", dans: *L'Investigateur. Journal de l'Institut historique*, 15ème année, t. 8, 1848.- p. 57-62 et 102-108.

BACHELOT, J.M. 1848c, "Notice sur le fût d'une colonne portant une inscription en caractères indiens et quelques figures en bas-relief", dans: *Revue archéologique ou recueil de document et de mémoires relatifs à l'étude des monuments, à la numismatique et à la phologie de l'antiquité et du Moyen-Âge, publiés par les princupaux archéologues français et étrangers*..., 4ème année, 2ème partie, 15 octobre 1847-15 mars 1848.- Paris, A. Leleux, 1848.- p. 456-459.

BACHELOT, J.M. 1850a, *Etudes archéologiques et géographiques mêlées d'observations et de notices diverses.*- Bruxelles, Librairie de Deprez-Parent, rue de la Violette, 15, F. Parent, éditeur, 1850.- in-8°, XIV + 536 p.

BACHELOT, J.M. 1850b, "Carte archéologione [sic] présentant la partie occidentale de la Gaule celtique, et la partie nord de l'Aquitaine sous les Romains, par le Bᵒⁿ de la Pylaie... 1848", dans: Bachelot 1850.- 1 carte dépliante, 34.000 "metres" to an inch, 374 x 515 mm, gravée sur pierre par E. Rembielinski.

LE MAOUT (Charles).- ed. 1851, *Bibliothèque bretonne. Collection de pièces inédites ou peu connues concernant l'histoire, l'archéologie et la littérature de l'ancienne province de Bretagne*, recueillies et publiée par Ch. Le Maout, imprimeur à Saint-Brieuc.- Saint-Brieuc, Le Maout, 1851.- 2 vol; [plusieurs notices de Bachelot].

BACHELOT, J.M. 1853, "Recherches archéologiques sur l'abbaye de Saint-Benoît et sur les antiquités de la contrée", dans: *Mémoires de la Société d'agriculture, sciences, belles-lettres, belles-lettres et arts de l'Orléanais*, t. 1, 1853.- p. 156.

BACHELOT, J.M. 1956, "Bachelot de la Pylaie. Extrait de *Archéologie celtique du Département d'Ille-et-Vilaine*", dans: *Bulletin et mémoires de la Société archéologique et historique de l'arrondissement de Fougères*, t. 1 [1956].- 37-39.

BACHELOT, J.M. 1973-1974, "Voyage à Houat en 1824", extraits de: *Essai sur la statistique des îles de Houat et d'Hédic*", dans: *Trouz-er-Mor* (Bulletin paroissial de Houat), n° 34 à 38, 1973-1974.

BACHELOT, J.M. 1975, "Edifices de construction romaine découverts dans le département d'Ille et Vilaine en 1830. I Le bourg de domagné et la chapelle de Saint-André. II Les tombeaux", dans: *Archéologie en Bretagne. Bulletin d'information de la Direction des Antiquités Historiques de Bretagne*, n° 4, septembre 1974.- p. 3-6.

BACHELOT, J.M. 1975, "Derniers restes de l'ancien temple romain situé en Saint-Just, au pied de la butte de Cojou, du côté du nord", dans: *Archéologie en Bretagne, Bulletin d'information de la Direction des Antiquités Historiques de Bretagne*, n° 5, 1ᵉʳ trimestre.- p. 3-4.

BACHELOT, J.M. 1975, "Les excursions archéologiques du baron de la Pylaie. Edifices de construction romaine découverts dans le département d'Ille-et-Vilaine en 1830. Langon et ses divers monuments. Butte de la Bosse ou du Chatel", édité par René Sanquer, dans: *Archéologie en Bretagne, Bulletin d'information de la direction des Antiquités Historiques de Bretagne*, n° 6, 2ème trimestre 1975.- p. 3-6.

BACHELOT, J.M. 1975, "Les excursions archéologiques du Baron de la Pylaie. Edifices de construction romaine découvert dans le département d'Ille et

Vilaine en 1830. III. Petit temple de Vénus devenu la chapelle de Sainte-Agathe à Langon sur la Vilaine", édité par René Sanquer, dans: *Archéologie en Bretagne, Bulletin d'information de la direction des Antiquités Historiques de Bretagne*, n° 7, 3ème trimestre.- p. 1-7.

BACHELOT, J.M. 1975, "Les excursions archéologiques du Baron de la Pylaie. IV. Quelques fortifications de terre du département d'Ille-et-Vilaine", édité par René Sanquer, dans: *Archéologie en Bretagne, Bulletin d'information de la direction des Antiquités Historiques de Bretagne*, n° 8, 4ème trimestre.- p. 9-12, 5 fig.

BACHELOT, J.M. 1976, "Les excursions archéologiques du Baron de la Pylaie. I – Recherches géographiques et historiques faites en 1835 sur la position de l'ancienne ville gauloise appelée corbilo", édité par René Sanquer, dans: *Archéologie en Bretagne, Bulletin d'information de la Direction des Antiquités Historiques de Bretagne*, n° 9, 1er trimestre 1976, p. 5-8, 2 notes bibliographiques in fine.

BACHELOT, J.M. 1976, "B – Les excursions archéologiques du Baron de la Pylaie: une monnaie gauloise découverte au 'cimetière aux huguenots' sur la lande de Langon (I.-et-V.)", édité par René Sanquer, dans: *Archéologie en Bretagne, Bulletin d'information de la Direction des Antiquités Historiques de Bretagne*, n° 9, 1er trimestre 1976, p. 18, 1 notes infra.

BACHELOT, J.M. 1976, "Les excursions archéologiques du Baron de la Pylaie. Rezé ou l'ancienne Corbilo", édité par René Sanquer, dans: *Archéologie en Bretagne, Bulletin d'information de la Direction des Antiquités Historiques de Bretagne*, n° 10, 2ème trimestre 1976, p. 1-10, 2 plans, 16 notes terminales par R. Sanquer.

BACHELOT, J.M. 1976, "Les excursions archéologiques du Baron de la Pylaie. Rezé ou l'ancienne Corbilo (suite)", édité par René Sanquer, dans: *Archéologie en Bretagne, Bulletin d'information de la Direction des Antiquités Historiques de Bretagne*, n° 11, 3ème trimestre 1976, p. 3-6.

BACHELOT, J.M. 1976, "Les excursions archéologiques du Baron de la Pylaie. Saint-Père-en-Retz, l'ancien Ratiatum, chef lieu du pays de Retz", édité par René Sanquer, dans: *Archéologie en Bretagne, Bulletin d'information de la Direction des Antiquités Historiques de Bretagne*, n° 12, 4ème trimestre 1976, p. 3-9, 3 notes terminales de Bachelot.

BACHELOT, J.M. 1977, "Les excursions archéologiques du Baron de la Pylaie. Les environs de Fougère: I / Monuments druidiques de la commune de Monthaut", édité par René Sanquer, dans: *Archéologie en Bretagne, Bulletin d'information de la Direction des Antiquités Historiques de Bretagne*, n° 13, 1er trimestre 1977, p. 7-11, 3 notes infra de Bachelot.

BACHELOT, J.M. 1977, "Dessins de monnaies joints aux textes de Bachelot de la Pylaie", édité par René Sanquer, dans: *Archéologie en Bretagne, Bulletin d'information de la Direction des Antiquités Historiques de Bretagne*, n° 14, 2ème trimestre 1977, p. 16, 1 notes infra de la rédaction.

BACHELOT, J.M. 1977, "Les excursions archéologiques du Baron de la Pylaie. Les environs de Fougère: II / Camp gaulois nommé le camp de l'étang des Châteaux / Tertre de Pierre-Laye et chemin de la Duchesse Anne / Chemin de la Duchesse Anne", édité par René Sanquer, dans: *Archéologie en Bretagne, Bulletin d'information de la Direction des Antiquités Historiques de Bretagne*, n° 15, 3ème trimestre 1977, p. 1-4.

BACHELOT, J.M. 1977, "Les excursions archéologiques du Baron de la Pylaie. Excursion archéologique à Jublains en 1934", édité par René Sanquer, dans: *Archéologie en Bretagne, Bulletin d'information de la Direction des Antiquités Historiques de Bretagne*, n° 16, 4ème trimestre 1977, p. 3-9, 1 note infra.

BACHELOT, J.M. 1977, "Fig. 17 – Chenêts d'argile à tête de bélier, découvert dans le canal de l'Erdre en 1813 (d'après un dessin de Bachelot de la Pylaie)", édité par René Sanquer, dans: *Archéologie en Bretagne, Bulletin d'information de la Direction des Antiquités Historiques de Bretagne*, n° 17, 1er trimestre 1978.- p. 36.

BACHELOT, J.M. 1977, "Les excursions archéologiques du Baron de la Pylaie", édité par René Sanquer, dans: *Archéologie en Bretagne, Bulletin d'information de la Direction des Antiquités Historiques de Bretagne*, n° 18, 2ème trimestre 1978, p. 1-10, 1 fig., 3 notes infra. de Bachelot.

BACHELOT, J.M. 1982, "Sur une découverte du baron de la Pylaie en 1845 à Saint-Pierre-Quilbignonc", dans: *Les Cahiers de l'Iroise*, janvier-mars 1982.- p. 30-32.

BACHELOT, J.M. 2004, *Jean-Marie Bachelot de la Pylaie. Voyage d'un naturaliste dans les îles d'Houat et d'Hédic 1825-1826*. Présenté par Pierre Butin. Préface de Gérard Aymonin.- Hoëdic, Melvan / Bibliothèque centrale du Muséum nationale d'histoire naturelle, 2004.- 174 p., cartes fac-sim., couv. ill., 24 cm.- ISBN: 2-9520979-0-9.

THE *VIDEDYS* LONG DOLMEN 1643-2006

Torben DEHN

Kulturarvsstyrelsen, H.C. Andersens Boulevard 2, DK 1553 Copenhagen K, Denmark

Translation from Danish: Anne Bloch & David Robinson

Abstract: This paper identifies a megalithic monument, used as a motif in drawings from 1643 and 1763, as the Videdys long dolmen in the Birkede area on the island Sealand, Denmark. The drawings are compared with later depictions and constructional details are analysed. The history of Videdys and two other dolmens in the area is recounted.
Key words: Antiquarian, Dolmen, Megalith, Videdys

Résumé: Cet article établit l'identité d'un monument mégalithique, utilisé comme motif dans des dessins de 1643 et 1763, comme le dolmen long Videdys dans la région de Birkede dans l'île Sealand, au Danemark. Les dessins sont comparés avec des représentations ultérieures et les détails de construction sont analysés. L'histoire de Videdys et de deux autres dolmens dans cette région est racontée.
Mots-clés: antiquaire, dolmen, mégalithe, Videdys

The first international archaeological congress was held in Neuchâtel in Switzerland in 1866, and in August 1869 the fourth congress was held in Copenhagen, Denmark, in order to discuss, among other things, the Danish kitchen middens. The international participants came mainly from Sweden and France, but Germany was also well represented. The Stone Age was the dominant theme at the congress; half the programme was devoted to this subject and one of the excursions was to the Sølager kitchen midden, while another had some megalithic graves as its subject (Wiell 1997).

Some of the participants, however, had already seen several examples of Danish megalithic architecture on their journey to Copenhagen. They had taken the train across Zealand and in Birkede Skov, about 50 km from Copenhagen, the train stopped so that the passengers could appreciate two megalithic tombs which lay immediately alongside the railway track in a small beech forest – in the words of a Danish news magazine covering the event: *"the first triumphal arch where prehistory itself bid them welcome"*

And these words were very appropriate in several respects. The monuments that the travellers could see from the train belong to a group of megalithic tombs that are among the first prehistoric monuments to be described in Danish archaeology. On one side of the railway, up on a hill, lay the 16 m long long barrow Kælderbakken (literally "Cellar Hill") with large kerbstones and a great capstone visible. On the other side lay the 52 m long barrow Langben Rises Høj ("The Long-legged Giant's Mound"; Riese = "giant" in German) with unusually large kerbstones less than 10 m from the railway tracks. One of the earliest known Danish archaeological investigations was carried out in this barrow.

It was the Rector of Copenhagen University, Erasmus Enewold Brochmand who, in 1658, let *"the earth open and found under a dome of boulders an urn with ash together with some bones"*. In this *"burial place ... on Daastrup Mark the renowned giant Lange Beenriser is thought to be interred"*. The information about Dåstrup parish, within which Birkede lies, is given in Pontoppidan's topographical work of 1763 *Den Danske Atlas* (The Danish Atlas). This was only one of several investigations, as at least 120 archaeologically-motivated excavations are known from the period between 1500 and 1800 (Randsborg 1994, fig. 11 and Appendix E).

However, one of the other barrows in Birkede was described as early as 1643. In 1638-39 local clergymen were required to report anything of antiquarian interest within their districts. This initiative was taken by Ole Worm (1588-1654), professor, medical scientist and founder of the Museum Wormianum which had runic stones as its speciality. Unfortunately the reports received from the local clergy were damaged by a great fire in Copenhagen. However, in Worm's *Danicorum Monumentorum Libri Sex* from 1643 there is an illustration of a dolmen. This work deals mostly with runic stones, and the only information given concerning this monument is the name of the site: *Birkede*.

120 years later, in 1763, Professor Erich Pontoppidan published his Danish Atlas, a topographic work containing descriptions of the landscape, animals, plants and history. Archaeology was of special interest to Pontoppidan. He regarded the barrows *"as a kind of archive which most wisely let us reach conclusions concerning our ancestors' way of life"*. In his great work of 1763, Pontoppidan used prefects, i.e. administrative heads of the regions, as informants but he was also a very experienced archaeologist himself. In Pontoppidan's work we again find Worm's dolmen from Birkede, but reproduced in a "contemporary" artistic style.

Pontoppidan's later copy is just a "modernised" version and its value as a source is limited. The original from 1643 is an idealised depiction but with some remarkable

Fig. 4.1. The megalithic tombs on each side of the rails in Birkede Skov:
a) Kælderbakken in 1887 and b) Langben Rises Høj in 2005. Photo: T. Dehn

Fig. 4.2. Illustration from O. Worm: *Danicorum Monumentorum Libri Sex*, 1643

Fig. 4.3. Illustration from E. Pontoppidan: *Den Danske Atlas I*, 1763

details. We do not know if the artist had seen the monument for himself or if he was working on the basis of sketches or verbal information. However, we do know that megalithic monuments were, during this period, in a much better state of preservation than at the end of the 19th century, after stones had been plundered for use as building material. The circles of stones around the chambers and the other stones within the rectangular setting belong to the structure of the barrow, and are visible due to the partially decayed earthen mounds. We find these circles and lines of stones when excavating within the barrows today; they mark out sections of the mound during the building process.

These stones, visible at the surface of the mounds, are often described in reports received from the local clergymen in the period from 1808-10. A Royal Commission was set up in 1807, one of whose tasks was to select those ancient monuments which should be preserved for posterity. Again, it was the clergymen from each parish who had to report to *The Royal Commission for the Preservation of Ancient Monuments*, giving information about the existing ancient monuments. The Commission then chose those worthy of preservation. These reports did, of course, vary greatly in quality but, collectively, they give a unique picture of the landscape at that time and of the appearance and location of the ancient monuments – especially megalithic graves – in the landscape (Adamsen & Jensen 1995-98). When all the reports had been examined the Commission designated a total of 231 ancient monuments within the then borders of Denmark, of which about 75% were megalithic structures.

However, one of the members of the Commission, Børge Thorlacius (1774-1829) Professor of Classical Philology, knew of the reference in *Den Danske Atlas* to Langben Rises Høj and in August 1808 travelled to Dåstrup parish to inspect the famous monument for himself (Adamsen & Jensen 1998, pp. 82-84; Jakobsen 2007, p. 26). Under the guidance of two local clergymen he discovered that there were several (six, in fact) barrows in the area around Birkede. And within an area of about 4 x 5 km in Dåstrup parish, of which Birkede is part, there is information on about 33 megalithic tombs, of which two thirds still

Fig. 4.4. a,b,c,d,e: Videdys. The National Museum's survey from 1887 and photograph after restoration in 1937, plus two photographs from 2005. Photo 1937: The National Museum, 2005: T. Dehn

survive to some degree. Only two of these are passage graves, and the rest are round dolmens and, in particular, long barrows. This is quite a dense concentration which lies in isolation relative to the other megalithic tombs in the region. Thorlacius visited a number of them and decided that attempts should be made to preserve four of them.

Of these four, one cannot be identified today, the second is the long barrow Kælderbakken, now disappeared – see below – the third is the above-mentioned Langben Rises Høj, but the fourth is a long barrow by the name of Videdys. The name "Vide-dys" refers to "Vide", i.e. the "Videric" who killed Langben Rise (the "long-legged giant") who lies buried in the above-mentioned long barrow of the same name. Thorlacius calls Videdys majestic because of its size and its location in the landscape as it *"with its mass awakens a kind of holy reverence in the passing traveller"*.

Thorlacius was clearly impressed by Videdys and its favourable state of preservation and concludes his description with a remark to the effect that not a word is mentioned about it in Pontoppidan's *Den Danske Atlas*.

This is, however, incorrect because Videdys is probably the very dolmen that is depicted in both *Den Danske Atlas* and Worm's 120-year earlier work. In support of this conclusion are the name of the locality, Birket or Birkede, and the monument's characteristic form, with a dome-shaped mound or elevation at each end within the kerbstones.

In 1887 A.P. Madsen surveyed Videdys for the National Museum. He drew a ground plan and a longitudinal profile of "Videdysse". A number of characteristic features can be recognised here which point in the direction of Worm's illustration, with the exception of one detail, the great mound in the middle, on which stands the chamber. Conversely there is, at each end of the frame of kerbstones, an elevated area with stones at its foot; the chamber has only three orthostats and a row of stones has been exposed between the chamber and one of the elevated areas. The latter are the characteristic features that can be seen on Worm's drawing, together with the information that it lies at Birkede. Demolition of the barrow had already begun in 1887 as the plan drawing shows a few split and cleaved stones, including the mound's southernmost kerbstones, which are those closest to an access road.

If Worm's and Pontoppidan's illustrations and information from 1643 and 1763 are compared with A.P. Madsen's from 1887, everything indicates that it is one and the same long dolmen, i.e. Videdysse/Videdys. First and foremost, there is the location given as "at Birkede" in Dåstrup parish. Birkede is the name of a small delimited area with few farms and houses, from where there is information concerning a further six barrows which can be termed in the same way. However, none of these bears the slightest resemblance to the long barrow in the illustrations. Then there are some coincidences between characteristic elements on Worm's and A.P. Madsen's illustrations, which – apart from the results of a restoration in 1937 – correspond with its appearance today.

One example comprises the two transverse rows of stones which, on the ground plan from 1887, can be seen on either side of the chamber. These could be remains of sectional divisions within the long barrow or support stones for the packing surrounding the chamber. Closer examination of the drawing from 1643 reveals that the stones in front of the three mounds do not lie in a straight line but more probably make up three circles, one around each mound. This is seen most clearly on the drawing from 1643 but can also just be perceived on that from 1763.

A very obvious difference is, as already mentioned, the great mound on which the chamber stands. This is seen neither on A.P. Madsen's drawing from 1887 nor in reality. One explanation could be that the 17th century artist did not visit the locality for himself but worked from sketches and verbal descriptions which he misunderstood. The form of the chamber and its location on top of a large domed mound, surrounded by one or more stone circles, is a standard depiction seen in several later illustrations. At that time it was not considered possible that a dolmen chamber could stand on flat terrain, but only on the top of a mound. Part of the explanation is apparent from the terminology, in that the word "dysse" (= dolmen) was used for the whole structure, whereas the chamber was termed a (stone) altar. And an altar, by the very nature of things, stands raised above its surroundings. It is apparent from Thorlacius' report that this perception of a dolmen chamber as a raised stone altar still applied 165 years later. Following his description of the large stones he explains the missing mound with the words: *The mound has, probably due to the weight of these, sunk at this place*. He is, for the same reason, in doubt concerning Videdys as a grave for Videric, because there is no trace of a stone cist (Adamsen & Jensen 1998, pp. 82f). It was not until 1843 that J.J.A. Worsaae effectively dismissed this perception of dolmens as altars and things (meeting places; Worsaae 1843).

Another explanation for the fact that the stones shown on the drawing from 1643 stand on a mound could be that, in the 17th century when decay was not so advanced, the chamber actually appeared as if it stood on a mound. This could then have disappeared prior to 1808 when Thorlacius described Videdys. If a little of the mound material around the chamber was preserved this could be perceived as a mound or an elevation. Today, we know that both dolmens and passage graves were built directly on the field surface – with or without topsoil – and that the mound was built up around and over the chamber and passage. Just above the level of the base of the mound around the chamber there can be various stone structures to stabilise the orthostats and it could be these that appeared during the mound's process of decay.

Videdys' later history includes the attempted breakage of a few kerbstones, but in 1937 it was lightly restored and again protected. Despite these interventions it still has its characteristic two mounds, one at each end, but unfortunately now hidden by large trees.

The two barrows that formed the triumphal arch for the congress participants in 1869 unfortunately no longer form a gateway. The round dolmen Langben Rises Høj is still an impressive sight for the thousands of train travellers between Copenhagen and Storebelt who pass it each day. But where the long barrow Kælderbakken lay there is now just a large crater in the hillside. When the railway was expanded in 1887, the dolmens' stones were broken into small pieces and laid between the sleepers and the earth beneath them was used to make the railway embankment. However, these actions created such a scandal and furore among travellers and politicians that the state railway's right to use ancient monuments for this purpose was annulled.

Fig. 4.5. Here lay the long barrow Kælderbakken until 1887 when it was used as fill under the railway tracks. Photo: T. Dehn

References

ADAMSEN, C. & JENSEN, V. (1995-1998) *Danske præsters indberetninger til Oldsagskommissionen af 1807*. Højbjerg.

JAKOBSEN, T.B. (2007) Birth of a World Museum. *Acta Archaeologica Vol. 78:1. Acta Archaeologica Supplementa* VIII. Oxford.

PONTOPPIDAN, E. (1763) *Den Danske Atlas I*. Copenhagen.

RANDSBORG, K. (1994) Ole Worm. An Essay in the Modernization of Antiquity. *Acta Archaeologica* 65, p. 135-169.

WIELL, S. (1997) 4. Internationale Antropologi- og Arkæologikongres i København 1869 – bag kulissen. *Aarbøger for Nordisk Oldkyndighed og Historie* 1996, p. 113-148.

WORM, O. (1643) *Danicorum Monumentorum Libri Sex. E spissis antiquitatum tenebis et in Dania ac Norvegia extantibus ruderibus eruti ab Olao Worm. D. Medicinae in Acad. Haffn. Professore publ. Hafniae*. Copenhagen.

WORSAAE, J.C.C. (1843) *Danmarks Oldtid oplyst med Oldsager og Gravhøje*. Copenhagen.

RESEARCH HISTORY OF THE ALTMARK MEGALITHIC TOMBS

Barbara FRITSCH

Landesamt für Denkmalpflege und Archäologie Sachsen-Anhalt, Richard-Wagner-Str. 9,
D-06114 Halle/Saale, Germany

Abstract: *The megaliths of the Altmark region have been known in literature since at least 16th century, with the early interpretations viewing them as burial places of historical heroes. Scientific excavations and first classifications date from the early 19th century. Since the megaliths were private property this was also the time of intensive destruction through agricultural developments; the fascination of the Romantics provides images of long destroyed monuments.*
Key words: *Altmark, antiquarians, megaliths*

Résumé: *Les mégalithes de la région de l'Altmark sont connus dans la littérature depuis le 16ème siècle au moins, avec les anciennes interprétations les voyant comme des lieus de sépulture de héros historiques. Les fouilles scientifiques et les premières classifications remontent au début du 19ème siècle. Comme les mégalithes étaient des biens personnels, c'était aussi l'époque de destructions intensives liées aux développements agricoles; la fascination des Romantiques fournit des images de monuments détruits depuis longtemps.*
Mots-clés: *Altmark, antiquaire, mégalithes*

INTRODUCTION

The Altmark region, situated approximately between the cities of Berlin and Hanover, is a part of the North European Plain (Fig. 5.1). The landscape is dominated by the ground and terminal moraines of the Saale-Weichsel glaciation, with glacial sander and areas of the younger Quaternary drained by tributaries of the Elbe. The landscape is gently undulating, with only the hills in the south-west Altmark reaching altitudes up to 160 m above sea level. Nowadays the Altmark region is sparsely populated, partly as a result of its former location at the inner-German border.

With regard to the megaliths, the Altmark represents the southernmost boundary of the distribution of dolmens in Central Europe and the southernmost distribution of the TRB culture (*Trichterbecherkultur*) passage graves. Apart from the group near Haldensleben – Bebertal – Marienborn, where 96 of the original 165 known graves are still preserved in one way or another, there are only a few megaliths known south of the area under consideration here, and these are found near the loess plains of Magdeburg (the so-called Mittelelbe-Saale region; Fischer 1956, 68ff.; Beier 1991)

At present there are 210 megalithic graves known in the Altmark region, of which 47 are still visible in the landscape. The remaining 163 monuments can still be located thanks to various reports of the past 250 years (Bock *et al.* 2006). Furthermore, there are 56 sites with scatters of flints or Tiefstich pottery which probably belong to domestic sites of the Late Neolithic. Thus the Altmark yields both domestic and funeral sites of the period between 3500 and 3000/2800 BC. While the overall distribution pattern suggests a shift from burial to domestic sites from west to east (Fig. 5.2), a survey of a small test region confirms the close proximity of both megaliths and domestic sites in the western Altmark.

RESEARCH HISTORY

The life of medieval rural populations was characterised by Christian mysticism and devoutness. Outstanding and conspicuous non-Christian structures such as megaliths were regarded as supernatural structures or some sort of sacrificial altars. However, since at least the 16th century onwards, the natives of the Altmark understood that megaliths were man-made structures in which ancestors were buried. Magister Christoph Entzelt (parson of Osterburg, born at Saalfeld near Salzwedel) mentioned a megalithic tomb near the small village of Stapel in his chronicle of the Altmark dated 1579. He reported that "big old men" were buried here (Entzelt 1579).

Research into megaliths began after the Reformation and intensified during the Age of Enlightenment, in the 17th-18th centuries, when social attitudes were changing. This pre-scientific exploration of the megaliths started also in the Altmark. The earliest evidence dates to 1741, when the parson of Bombeck described the first excavation of a megalithic chamber near Bierstedt. The former chief administrator of the Altmark, Wilhelm Ludewig von dem Knesebeck, permitted the excavation of some megaliths in 1728. Partly decorated pottery sherds, flint, ashes and human bones were found, and thus he concluded that the megaliths were graves of heroes or grand masters (Fritsch and Mittag 2006).

In 1751 Bernhard Ludwig Bekmann completed and published a manuscript of his deceased brother, Johann Christoph Bekmann, the „Historische Beschreibung der Chur und Mark Brandenburg". In its second part they described several "Antiquities of the Mark" including 36 megaliths, 12 of which were depicted by the Berlin copperplate engraver F.E. Gericke (Fig. 5.3). The two brothers differentiated between "Hünenbetten" and "sacrificial altars". They assumed that the surrounding stones of the megaliths had already been removed.

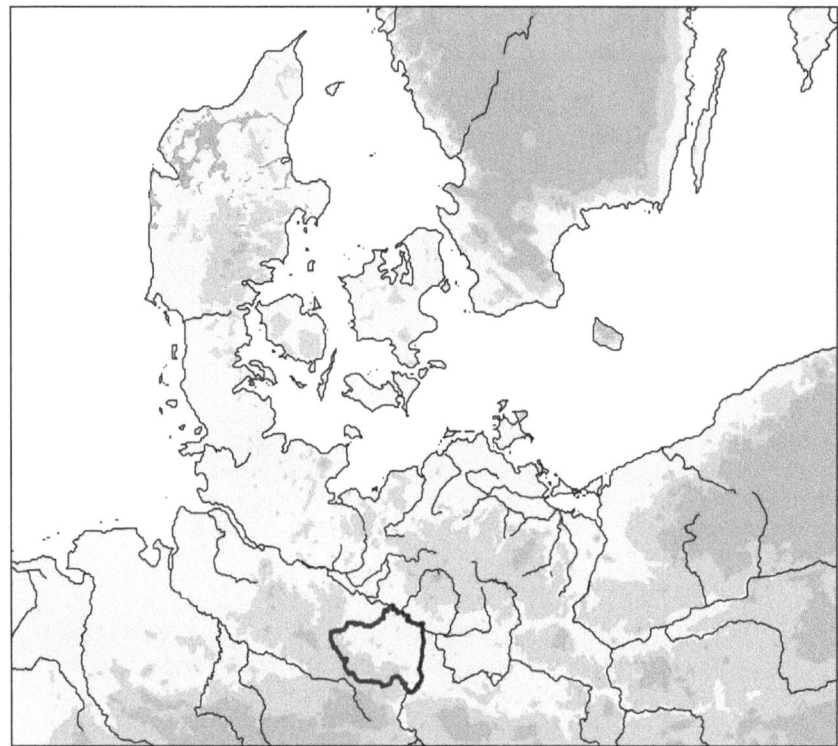

Fig. 5.1. Geographical situation of the Altmark

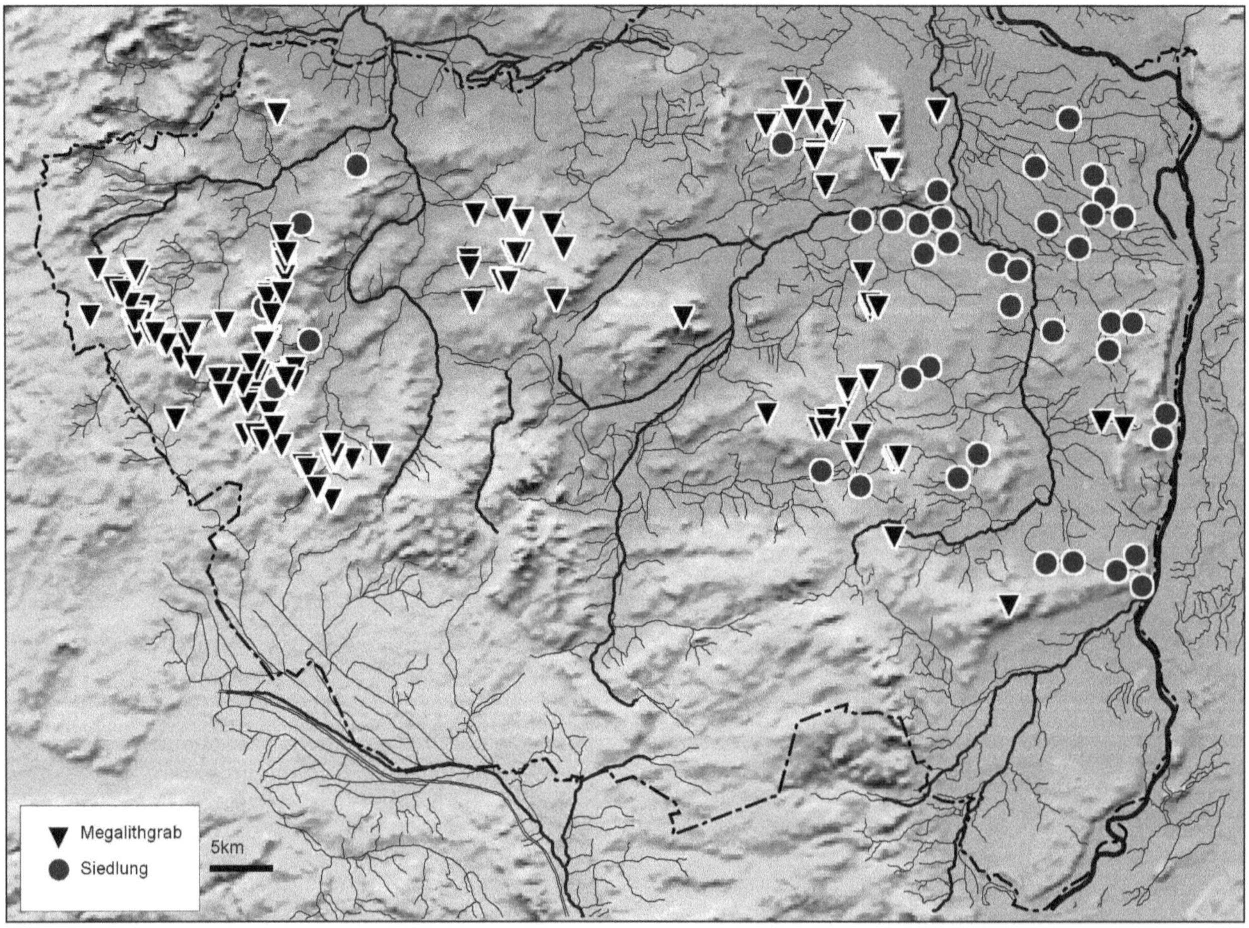

Fig. 5.2. Distribution of megalithic graves and Neolithic settlements in the Altmark
(triangle: megalithic grave, circle: settlement)

Fig. 5.3. Megalithic graves of Diesdorf (I and II), Hasselt (N. III) and Bretsch (IV and V), published by Gerike 1751 (Bekmann / Bekmann 1751, table II); only Diesdorf II (Salzwedel) is still preserved

The first scientific survey of the megaliths was undertaken by the famous school director from Salzwedel, Johann Friedrich Danneil. From 1820 until the 1840s he undertook many excavations – not only of megaliths – in the Altmark. He summarised his results in a general report about his excavations published in 1838 (Danneil 1838), at approximately the same time as Christian Thomsen, the founder of the Three Age System, and Friedrich Lisch, the famous Mecklenburg scientist, were publishing their work. Danneil identified three main groups of graves:

1. Hunebeds with only a few artefacts: single ceramic sherds, seldom a whole urn, and a single axe of flint or other stone.

2. Grave-mounds which he divided into two subgroups: the first contained urns with tools made of copper (bronze) but iron was (mostly) missing. The second group contained bronze as well as iron objects. Therefore, in the opinion of Danneil, they belonged to a younger time.

3. Graves without artificial mounds in which iron artefacts dominated.

Danneil's paper was the first publication in which the classification of graves and associated finds was based exclusively on excavations and on contextual observations. Since he confined his work to local

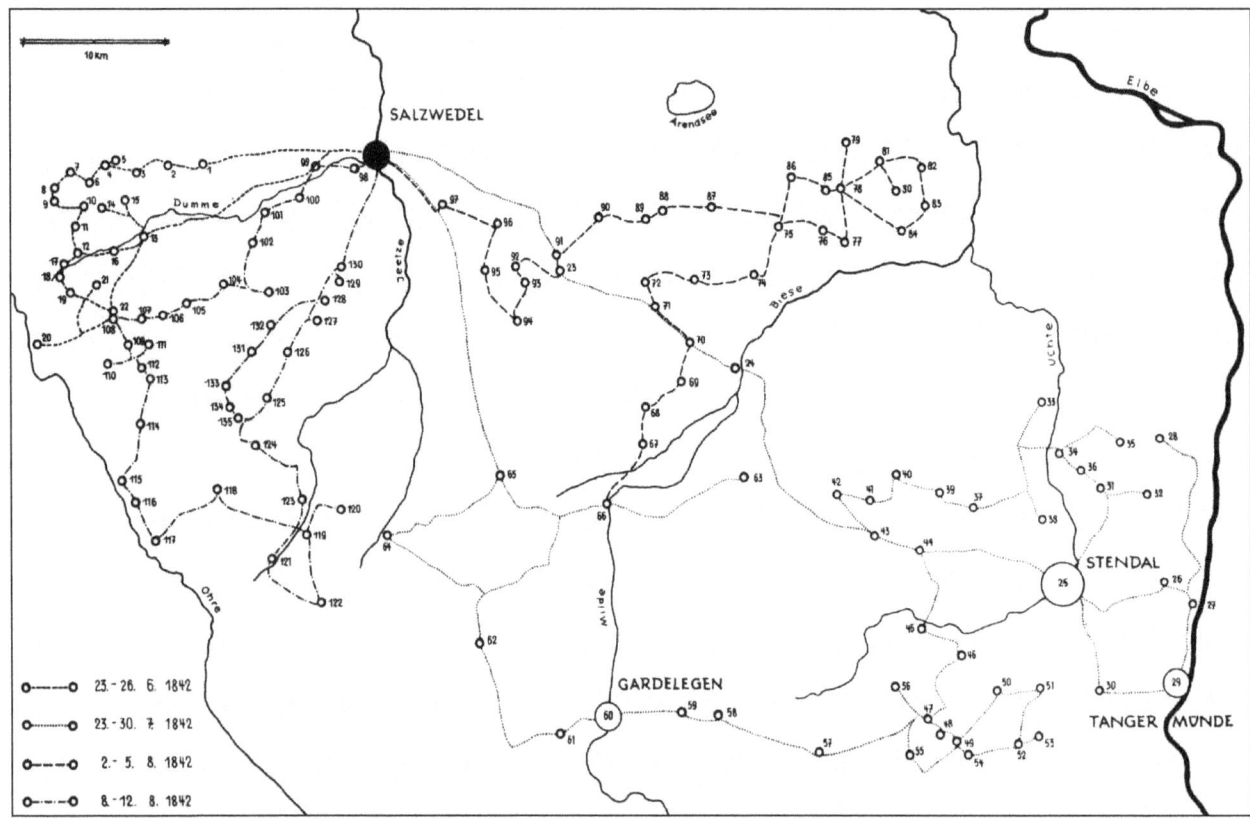

Fig. 5.4. J.F. Danneil's megalithic travel route in the Altmark, 23rd June to 12th August 1842 (Preuß 1983, 656 fig. 2)

prehistory, there was no further reaction to his general report.

In 1842 (23rd June – 12th August) Danneil travelled through the whole of the Altmark recording and describing all detectable megaliths (Fig. 5.4). His catalogue of 1843 listed 145 preserved graves. Danneil described 27 graves as "badly preserved", "not very good", "morbid" or similar, 100 were "well", "very well preserved", beautiful or similar (Danneil 1843).

Fifty years later, between 1888 and 1892, a new survey carried out by Eduard Krause, Conservator at the Royal Museum for Ethnography in Berlin, and Otto Schoetensack from Heidelberg, was published in 1893 in the *Zeitschrift für Ethnologie* (Fig. 5.5). On the basis of Danneil's and Bekmann's research, they listed and described 190 megaliths and mentioned 14 others. Plans accompanied the survey. Their report is still the main source for the reconstruction of spatial distribution of destroyed burial sites. A large number of photographs, which are stored mainly in the museums at Halle and Salzwedel, illustrate the surroundings of megaliths and the sites themselves. Only 50 megalithic graves or their remains had been preserved at that time, of which 45 were systematically surveyed and photographed. No more than 24 graves were still well or very well preserved, 9 were more or less destroyed, 15 existed only as ruins, two were destroyed during the survey, and 154 graves had been totally destroyed.

There has been no further scientific survey of the Altmark megaliths since 1893 although information about some of the graves was published occasionally during the 20th century. For example, the Salzwedel hospital director Walter Sudhoff took pictures and made drawings of the West Altmark megaliths at the beginning of the 1930s for an exhibition in Hamburg. The East Altmark monuments were described and published, together with much idealised drawings, in the books about the Monuments of Art of the Province of Saxony (1933, 1938).

Even Ernst Sprockhoff, who surveyed the megaliths of Germany during the 1920s and 1930s, was not able to work on the monuments of Sachsen-Anhalt, and so his "Atlas of the German Megaliths" only covered the territories of Schleswig-Holstein, Mecklenburg, Brandenburg, Pomerania, Lower Saxony and Westphalia.

A new survey was carried out in 1959 and 1960 by Dieter Kaufmann, Günter Wetzel and Walter Saal. The number of known megaliths in the Altmark then increased to over 200, but the results were not published. Another survey was conducted by Lothar Mittag and myself and was published in 2006 (Bock et al. 2006). We consulted old cadastral maps, descriptions, paintings and so on. Information, including characteristic features, on about 210 megalithic graves was recorded, although only 47 of these survive today. Only 19 of these megaliths can be described as very well or well preserved.

Fig. 5.5. E. Krause und O. Schoetensack during their researches in Lüdelsen, Altmarkkreis Salzwedel (Ortsakten LDA Halle/Saale)

Apart from documentation, hardly any new archaeological work took place on the Altmark megaliths during the 20th century. Besides smaller projects there has only been one larger investigation, namely that carried out by Ulrich Fischer, from the museum of Halle, in the years 1936-1938 (Fischer 1939; Preuss 1980, 101ff.). Near the small village of Leetze (Wötz) six megalithic graves are located, arranged in a north-south orientated row. Fischer excavated three monuments of which Leetze 1 and Leetze 6 are of greater interest. In Leetze 1, different floor layers were observed within the chamber and some finds were recorded from in front of the tomb. Due to the acid nature of the soils hardly any bones survived, except for part of a human skull. The radiocarbon date for this skull suggests that it belongs to a secondary burial from the late Neolithic, which demonstrates the interest that the Single Grave culture communities probably still showed in above-ground architecture. The pottery uncovered belongs to the Tiefstich ceramics, especially to the chronologically early Düsedau type. In general, no stratigraphy could be observed and no hints as to the burial rite were found, but a good deal of information with respect to the megalithic architecture was gathered. Similarly, the excavation of the passage grave (Leetze 6) led to the discovery of the Tiefstich ceramics – probably from the chronologically younger Haldensleben type – as well as the Globular Amphora culture pottery. Again, no stratigraphical order or hints for the reconstruction of the burial rite were observed.

Nevertheless, considering the excavations near Bebertal, south of the Altmark (Preuss 1973), younger monuments were probably larger in size than the older ones. Extended dolmens were probably being erected from about 3500 BC, whereas passage graves came into use around 3300 BC. Traditionally, the Düsedau horizon is linked with Brindley's stages 1 and 2 of the Western TRB, as well as with the MN Ia phase of the Northern TRB group; Haldensleben is associated with Brindley's stages 3 and 4, as well as with MN I b / II in the North. The distribution of the Tiefstich ceramics provides evidence for at least a communication network towards the Lower Elbe region in the northwest on the one hand, and to the south and southwest on the other. The distribution indicates a second centre of Tiefstich wares used by communities along the northern border of the central German loess area, right into the Köthen district between the Saale and the Mulde. Some Tiefstich imports are known from megalithic graves and other burial places in the south.

DESTRUCTION HISTORY

The widespread destruction of megaliths probably began some time after Christianisation. It was easier to build Christian churches next to such heathen places – we find an example in Winterfeld, Western Altmark, where a megalith was known in the rectory garden of a 13th-century church. This monument was not destroyed until the 19th century by the construction of a new stable.

As early as the middle of the 18th century, Johann Christian Bekmann complained that the farmers were removing the big stones. The greatest destructions occurred in the 19th century, as a result of the Reformation and the Age of Enlightenment.

As a result of the agrarian reforms of 1807 and 1811 the Altmark farmers could also buy themselves out from their dependency on landlords. Private farmland was now split and widely distributed throughout the district. This changed after the separation that led to the rearrangement of the agricultural land, when all farmers got their farmland in interrelated areas. Another reason for destruction was the progress in agriculture: owing to the new farming methods (use of artificial fertiliser) it was possible to till more and poorer soils. At the same time, as a result of industrialisation and the increasing population, people needed more building material. The big stones, once broken up, were quite suitable for the building of new streets, houses, stables or churches.

Danneil knew this. The principal aims of his investigations and of his survey of 1842 were, on the one hand, research and on the other hand the preservation of the megaliths of the Altmark. From correspondence between Danneil and the provincial authorities, we know about his tireless but unsuccessful activities to protect the graves. Although the authorities understood the urgency of the situation, it was not possible to protect the megaliths: there existed no law against the destruction of hunebeds. Like many other monuments they were private, not public property. Nearly two-thirds of the megaliths were destroyed during the 50 years following Danneil's interventions. Theodor Zechlin confirmed the destruction of many graves for stone extraction in 1862 (Zechlin 1863, 6f.). Johann Joachim Matthias, a former citizen of Tangeln in the Altmark, visited his home town for the last time in 1893 and noted that most of the Tangeln megaliths – as he remembered them – were gone. So he painted a retrospective picture, evoking the megaliths as they were in 1846, when he was a young man, as a kind of protest against the harm done to the monuments.

Further destruction, although of a lesser extent, took place after 1893. Only four megaliths, described by Krause and Schoetensack as more or less preserved, are missing today. Having said this, only 19 monuments are in good or very good condition today, whereas 8 are badly damaged and 163 have disappeared completely. While on the one hand this is an immeasurable loss of cultural heritage, on the other hand the percentage of surviving objects is still relatively high. In the eastern part of the Altmark, where industrial agriculture was practised, most of the monuments were lost.

Megaliths as monuments have attracted people for centuries – in the Altmark as well as in many other regions of Europe. The modern scientific view of the megaliths is but one way of dealing with these monuments. Like our ancestors we are unable to look at megaliths without dealing with them in our own way. In every age they have forced people to react to them – because of their monumentality and their outstanding appearance.

We do not know what people of the past thought or what social systems operated in prehistory, but we do know they also regarded the megaliths as something special. Since the time of the Single Grave Culture, we know of several prehistoric and early historic secondary burials. We also know that many capstones and so-called "guard stones" at the end of the hunebeds, as well as the big, solitary erratic blocks show cupmarks. These cupmarks have been created since the Bronze Age, but we also have evidence dating some of them to the Middle Ages.

In the Middle Ages and in early modern times, megaliths were seen as supernatural structures or as the works of giants (in German: Hünen – Hünenbetten), for example as sacrificial altars. The sketches and prints from the end of the nineteenth century illustrate the romantic fascination for both the well-known megalithic grave of Stöckheim and the Neolithic life. Despite this attitude many monuments were destroyed, especially around the time that such pictures were drawn. In this respect our scientific investigations into megaliths are only one of several ways of dealing with the unknown. Thus megaliths are an example of a general pattern of human behaviour: that of the wish and the need to control the unknown. And thus we discover, through our enquiries, an anthropological principle of human existence for all times.

References

BEIER, H.-J. (1991) *Die megalithischen, submegalithischen und pseudomegalithischen Bauten sowie die Menhire zwischen Ostsee und Thüringer Wald*. Wilkau-Haßlau (Beiträge zur Ur- und Frühgeschichte Mitteleuropas 1).

BEKMANN, J.Chr.; BEKMANN, B.L. (1751) *Historische Beschreibung der Chur und Mark Brandenburg*. Zweiter Teil: Von den Alterthümern der Mark. Berlin, p. 345-452.

BOCK, H.; FRITSCH, B.; MITTAG, L. (2006) *Großsteingräber der Altmark*. Halle (Saale): Landesamt für Denkmalpflege und Archäologie Sachsen-Anhalt.

DANNEIL, J.F. (1838) Grabalterthümer aus vorchristlicher Zeit; Eintheilung der verschiedenen Grabdenkmäler aus der heidnischen Zeit in der Altmark. *Erster Jahresbericht des Altmärkischen Vereins für vaterländische Geschichte und Industrie*, p. 31-57.

DANNEIL, J.F. (1843) Specielle Nachweisung der Hünengräber in der Altmark. *Sechster Jahresbericht des Altmärkischen Vereins für vaterländische Geschichte und Industrie*, p. 86-122.

ENTZELT (1579) *Magister Christoph Entzelts Chronicon der Altmark*. Stendal (1925): Facsimile-Ausgabe.

FISCHER, U. (1939) Großsteingrabuntersuchungen in der Altmark. *Jahresbericht des Altmärkischen Vereins für vaterländische Geschichte zu Salzwedel* 53, p. 3-8.

FISCHER, U. (1956) *Die Gräber der Steinzeit im Saalegebiet*. Vorgeschichtliche Forschungen 15. Berlin.

FRITSCH, B.; MITTAG, L. (2006) Forschungs- und Zerstörungsgeschichte. In: Bock, H.; Fritsch, B.; Mittag, L. – *Großsteingräber der Altmark*. Halle (Saale): Landesamt für Denkmalpflege und Archäologie Sachsen-Anhalt, p. 13-21.

KRAUSE, E.; SCHOETENSACK, O. (1893) Die megalithischen Gräber (Steinkammergräber) Deutschlands. I. Altmark. *Zeitschrift für Ethnologie* 25, p. 105-170.

PREUSS, J. (1973) Megalithgräber mit Alttiefstichkeramik im Haldensleber Forst. *Neolithische Studien* II, p. 127-208.

PREUSS, J. (1980) *Die altmärkische Gruppe der Tiefstichkeramik*. Berlin: Deutscher Verlag der Wissenschaften.

PREUSS, J. (1983) Johann Friedrich Danneil und die Großsteingräber der Altmark. *Ethnographisch-Archäologische Zeitschrift* 24, p. 649-667.

ZECHLIN, T. (1863) Jahresbericht – erstattet in der Generalversammlung vom 19. Dez. 1862. *Jahresbericht des Altmärkischen Vereins für vaterländische Geschichte und Industrie. Salzwedel* 13, p. 3-16.

NINETEENTH-CENTURY PORTUGUESE AT THE MEGALITHS

Ana Cristina MARTINS

Centre for Archaeology (UNIARQ), University of Lisbon

Abstract: Although later and less frequently than in other European countries closely involved in archaeological development, Portugal witnessed a growing interest in megalithic research. The monuments, especially the dolmens, were excavated, drawn, photographed and protected. Detailed studies, briefly explained in this paper, were part of a larger project relating megalithic studies to a wider nationalist archaeological agenda.
Key words: Megaliths, Portugal, nationalism

Résumé: Bien que plus tard, et moins fréquemment que dans d'autres pays européens étroitement impliqués dans le développement archéologique, le Portugal fut témoin d'un intérêt grandissant dans la recherche mégalithique. Les monuments, particulièrement les dolmens, furent fouillés, dessinés, photographiés, et protégés. Des études détaillées, expliquées brièvement dans cet article, firent partie d'un plus grand projet qui reliait l'étude des mégalithes à un programme archéologique national plus vaste.
Mots clés: Mégalithisme, Portugal, nationalisme

INTRODUCTION

During the nineteenth century, the birth and development of the discipline of archaeology in many European countries depended not only upon intellectual investment but also upon the role of archaeology within the broad nationalist movements. However, this cannot be said of archaeology in Portugal, where it did not play a role in the national process of studying and safeguarding the remains of the past. Indeed, against the background of the domestic problems evident from 1800 onwards, Portugal, in contrast to other countries, seemed to lack the historiographical, and by inference archaeological, bases to validate its ideological pretensions and, by extension, its territorial domains.

Against this background we may ask what was the role of archaeological activity, especially at a time when its scientific status had yet to be recognised. Indeed, in a nation where the political establishment did not have to rely upon a validation provided by remains uncovered through archaeological excavation, one might assume that archaeology was unnecessary. However, the situation was in fact more complex, as the presence of Phoenician, Greek and Roman remains in the territory of Portugal was recognised in the Royal Decree (Alvará; Fig. 6.1) issued in 1721 by the enlightened King João V (1706-1750), possibly at the instigation of the then recently formed Royal Academy of History (*Real Academia de História*) established in 1720.

Moreover the explanations, based on the mythical (biblical) foundation of *Tróia* (the nineteenth-century *Caetobriga*), or Setúbal, its neighbouring village, enter a domain of political objectives which benefited those dedicated to the study of the past, and filling a certain inner vacuum by providing answers to queries about the unknown.

This process took place during the 19th century, in a period characterised by a second renascence of the classical world, which placed in a privileged position the cultures of the Ancient Mediterranean and was used in the affirmation of a certain ideological supremacy whenever national borders had to be enlarged. Indeed, the 1800s brought a novelty: a past recovered by archaeological knowledge. We refer specifically to megalithic monuments, rapidly elevated to prominence by nations without the monuments characteristic of the past territories of the Roman Empire – a model which, more than that of the Republic of Pericles, became part of the political agendas of the second half of the nineteenth century.

In Portugal, however, there was no need to revert to such an ancient past, since the originality of its culture and the legitimisation of its boundaries had been defined in mediaeval times. Nevertheless, it is remarkable that it was precisely in the aftermath of the movement for the 'Iberian Union', and the decadent discourse emanating from the Portuguese intellectuals of the so-called 'Generation of '70' (*Geração de 70*), that megalithic studies found their ultimate path onto the agenda of the nation's thinkers. Possibly this served to justify the reasons behind the 'Union', precisely through the precedent of the prehistoric megalithic phenomenon in the national territory, by comparison with examples found on Spanish soil. This issue receded as soon as fears of an 'Iberian Union' disappeared.

While nineteenth-century archaeology sometimes assumed a crucial role in the processes of unification and/or reunification (as may be demonstrated in the case of Italy and Germany) this was less so in the case of Portugal where, in the nineteenth century, separatist or regional autonomous movements were not so pronounced. In Spain, for example, archaeological studies, together with geography, ethnicity or language, served such a purpose by creating an image of a nation symbolised by historical union in fulfilment of a role granted by a divine power.

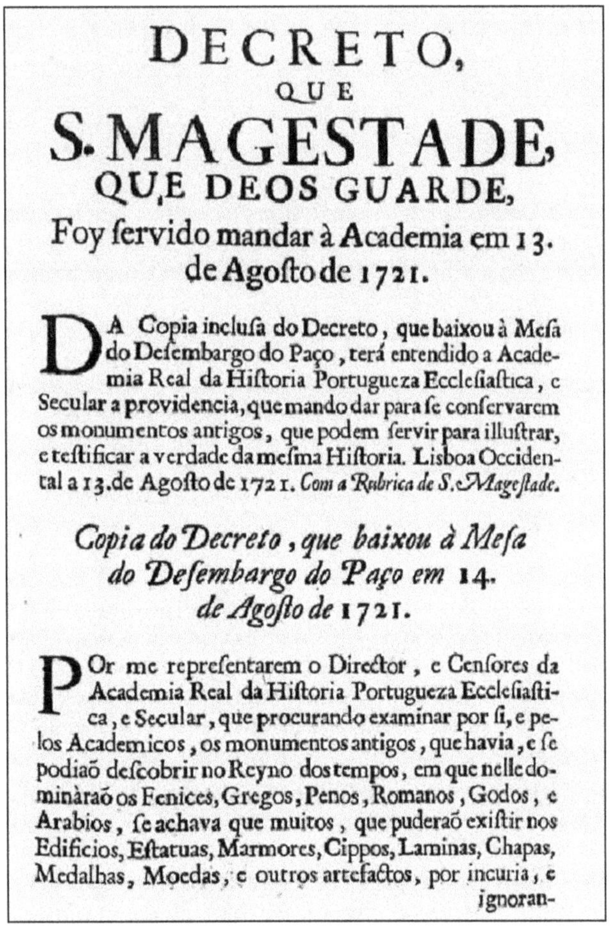

> DECRETO,
> QUE
> S. MAGESTADE,
> QUE DEOS GUARDE,
> Foy servido mandar à Academia em 13.
> de Agosto de 1721.
>
> DA Copia inclusa do Decreto, que baixou à Mesa do Desembargo do Paço, terá entendido a Academia Real da Historia Portugueza Ecclesiastica, e Secular a providencia, que mando dar para se conservarem os monumentos antigos, que podem servir para illustrar, e testificar a verdade da mesma Historia. Lisboa Occidental a 13. de Agosto de 1721. *Com a Rubrica de S. e Magestade.*
>
> *Copia do Decreto, que baixou à Mesa do Desembargo do Paço em 14. de Agosto de 1721.*
>
> POr me representarem o Director, e Censores da Academia Real da Historia Portugueza Ecclesiastica, e Secular, que procurando examinar por si, e pelos Academicos, os monumentos antigos, que havia, e se podiaõ descobrir no Reyno dos tempos, em que nelle dominàraõ os Fenices, Gregos, Penos, Romanos, Godos, e Arabios, se achava que muitos, que puderaõ existir nos Edificios, Estatuas, Marmores, Cippos, Laminas, Chapas, Medalhas, Moedas, e outros artefactos, por incuria, e ignoran-

Fig. 6.1. Royal Decree of 1721

THE STUDY OF PORTUGUESE MEGALITHS DURING THE NINETEENTH CENTURY

In Portugal, the lack of regional pro-autonomy factions may also be one of the reasons why we lack the visual images, so typical of French and English iconographies, of antiquarians portrayed next to megalithic and other ancient monuments. However, through the later 19th century fieldwork activities carried out on behalf of the Portuguese Geological Services (*Serviços Geológicos de Portugal*), the most popularly analysed megalithic types – dolmens – were included in the general category of prehistoric monuments, even if the already outdated concept of their being Celtic monuments persisted. In practice, the study of megaliths grew in popularity among Portuguese researchers who, moreover, subscribed to the pan-European Romantic spirit associated with their investigations.

Most relevant here was the fact that a geographical comparison of these structures was suggested through the analysis of their respective architectural typology. This was further underlined by the idea that

> "*more civilised nations do not refrain from the performance of their archaeological researches because they may be thought of as sublime*" (Silva 1888, 26), and that "*the different objects discovered during excavations conducted at those monuments, are now attributed to the first Prehistoric migrations, whose period and duration are unknown*"(Silva 1881, 69-71).

The scholars believed, therefore, that megaliths were built in the Portuguese territory as part of a diffusionist phenomenon. They valued archaeological research and engaged in it in a manner similar to that described by the eminent French prehistorian Émile Cartailhac (1845-1921), in *Les Âges Préhistoriques d'Espagne et du Portugal*, regarding the architectural megalithic types and associated assemblages as possible indicators of settlement evolution in a given region. With reference to this, one of the great and enthusiastic Portuguese scholars of megalithic studies, V. do M. Gabriel Pereira (1847-1911), stated that

> "*the dolmens of Évora are undoubtedly unique, and their study important towards the definition of the civilisation and relations between primitive peoples of this area, if attention is given to the differences seen between them and those from other areas [...] not so much in their construction, but in their position, [in relation to] objects found in the surrounding area*" (I.A.N./T.T., 1876, VIIIa, 8.ª, 1260).

Although Portuguese researchers were interested in a broad typological spectrum of the megalithic monuments, in reality dolmens always attracted greater curiosity even if, unfortunately, a greater number of them had been destroyed by landowners in order to use the stones in various rural developments, through re-using parts of or entire structures whose meaning was by now lost in time. This situation would eventually be overcome through education of the local populations at the time when survey missions were conducted in the field.

It is therefore not surprising that, from 1874 onwards, the Board of the Royal Association of Portuguese Archaeologists (*Real Associação dos Arqueólogos Portugueses*; Fig. 6.2) was requesting its members to undertake cartographic surveys and recording, by means of drawings or engravings, of such monuments in the areas of their residence (Id., 1885, XVI, 8.ª, 3320). Whereas a distribution map of Portuguese dolmens was made three years earlier, in 1871, by the General Board of Geological Works (*Direcção Geral dos Trabalhos Geológicos*), it was confined to the region of *Évora*. Thus there was a need to extend it to cover the entire area of Portugal, in a way analogous to that done in France. There, Alexandre Louis Joseph Bertrand (1820-1902), one of the pioneers of Gallo-Roman archaeology as well as the founder and first director of the famous Musée des Antiquités Nationales at Saint-Germain-en-Laye, mapped the megaliths in the entire area of Europe.

Additionally, and similarly to the 'Archaeological Map of the Algarve' (*Carta Arqueológica do Algarve*) of Sebastião Philippes Estácio Martins da Veiga (1828-

Fig. 6.2. Headquarters of the Royal Association of Portuguese Archaeologists
(Real Associação dos Arqueólogos Portugueses)

1891), these maps would provide a record of archaeological heritage essential to the development of a heritage consciousness. These were, therefore, privileged inventory documents, essential to the preservation of a "memory" and, at the same time, providing the first stage in the classification of the monuments essential for their future safeguarding. In the meantime, it was urgent to call attention to the need for such an investigation *"avant que le vandalisme n'ait détruit un plus grand nombre de ces anciennes constructions"* ("Discussion", 1873, p. 726).

THE DISSEMINATION OF PORTUGUESE MEGALITHIC STUDIES ABROAD

Based on all these investigations (Fig. 6.3), the President of the Royal Association, the architect and archaeologist J. Possidónio N. da Silva (1806-1896), undertook a comparative study which was published and presented during the 1879 *Congrès International d'Anthropologie et d'Archéologie Préhistorique*, taking place in Italy, France and Belgium. The paper was repeated that same year at the *Congrès de l'Association Française pour l'Avancement des Sciences*, which was established in 1872. This article inspired the Swedish archaeologist Oscar Montelius (1843-1921) to come to Lisbon in order to study some of the artefacts from the excavated dolmens, which were at that time exhibited at the Carmo Archaeological Museum (*Museu Archeologico do Carmo*) on behalf of the Royal Association. As a result of this visit, Montelius stated that the Portuguese archaeological studies were *"beaucoup plus avancés qu'en Espagne [et peuvent] nous donner la solution de bien des questions importantes relatives aux peuples des dolmens"*

(I.A.N./T.T., 1879, XI, 8.ª, 1767). In the interim, Possidónio da Silva consulted Émile Cartailhac on the method of classification to be adopted in the typological examination of standing stones.

Examining the building methods of dolmens extant in Portugal and Spain, some Portuguese scholars, following a linear evolutionary approach, concluded that the Portuguese monuments were chronologically earlier, since the stones used in the Spanish dolmens *"are more regular and remain in a position closer to the vertical concept"* (Melo, 1886, p. 121). Meanwhile, excavations conducted at the dolmens in *Alentejo* (South and South-Eastern Portugal) and the identification of others erected on the left margins of part of the Guadiana river (South-Eastern Portugal), showing their presence on Spanish territory, convinced Possidónio da Silva that *"on peut donc croire que les Celtes sont venus dans la péninsule Ibérique par la rive droite de la Guadiana"* (Silva, 1881, p. 620). Thus their precedence in Portugal was implied, even if their presence there resulted from a Celtic "migratory wave", the Celts being the people to whom the conception and building of dolmens was attributed: *"Cette circonstance doit servir beaucoup pour aider à faire les recherches pour trouver la marche que les Celtes auront prise pour entrer dans l'Europe"* ("Discussion", 1873, p. 726).

Alongside the illustrative and cartographic survey, members of the Royal Association of Portuguese Archaeologists were also requested to inventory the presence of the toponym *anta* – the term by which dolmens were known in Portugal – since in the Minho region, for example, *"il devait y avoir eu beaucoup de ces*

Fig. 6.3. Portuguese megalith published in the second half of the 19th century

constructions préhistoriques, parce qu'il y a plusieurs bougardes qui conservent le nom d'Antas." (Silva, 1881b, p. 620).

Furthermore, Charles Laurière, the charismatic member of the *Royal Society of Northern Antiquaries*, established in Copenhagen in 1825, suggested that

> "*Votre Carte des Dolmens du Portugal [...] soit accompagnée d'un texte explicatif, indiquant la nature et la place occupée par les divers objets trouvés à votre connaissance [...] et particulièrement ce qui manque dans presque toutes les descriptions de ce genre, les éléments nécessaires pour apprecier, par comparaison, l'âge des poteries, l'aser ou débris de vases, c'est-à-dire, la composition de la pâte, sa couleur, son genre de fabrication à la main ou au tour, le degré de cuisson, lorsqu'ils ont passé au four, la forme. Ce travail sera l'un des plus utiles pour résoudre définitivement la question de l'origine des antiques populations de l'Ibérie* (I.A.N./T.T., 1876, VIIIa, 8.ª, 1353).

PROTECTION OF MEGALITHS

Mapping the different Portuguese megalithic types and their associated unique artefacts (such as the engraved plaques; Fig. 6.4), Possidónio da Silva called the attention of all those responsible for megalithic studies to the importance of such research and the urgency of protection while, at the same time, increasing the awareness of provincial scholars of the importance of these monuments for local history. He also thought that the Central Government was responsible for

> "... *their good preservation, not only to avoid their destruction and loss of the potential that they represent, but also that they may be converted into productive capital for the Country in general, and a true and active element of prosperity for the lands that have them, since everywhere they form a powerful stimulus to the curiosity of travellers*" (Silva, 1888, p. 7).

In this way, it was hoped to capitalise on the cultural heritage as a source of national, regional and local revenue, incorporating this model into a general plan of tourist development for the country, especially the so-called "cultural tourism". These measures were urgent considering that

> "*If some of these antiquities have escaped persistent destruction continuing into the present, it is because the dust and the earth, lifted by storms and displaced by torrential rains over the centuries, have gathered upon these precious relics of a past greatness, thus hiding them entirely from the coveting gaze of destroyers as implacable as they are ignorant*" (*Ibidem*).

In fact, Possidónio da Silva considered that, in a manner similar to foreign examples, the most efficient way of stopping the destruction of megaliths lay in their classification as "national monuments" (A.H./A.A.P., *Actas da Assembleia Geral*, 132, 7/4/1889; Id., *Idem*, 137, 22/12/1889). For this reason it was necessary to complete their exhaustive inventory, emphasising their distinct character in comparison with those found in other countries.

This seemed all the more interesting, since it indicated the absence of a relationship between the contemporary realities observed in a given geographical-mental space and the requirements of perception of remote periods, identified in the same area. Moreover, it was typical of the general tendency of the period to (re-)encounter the past

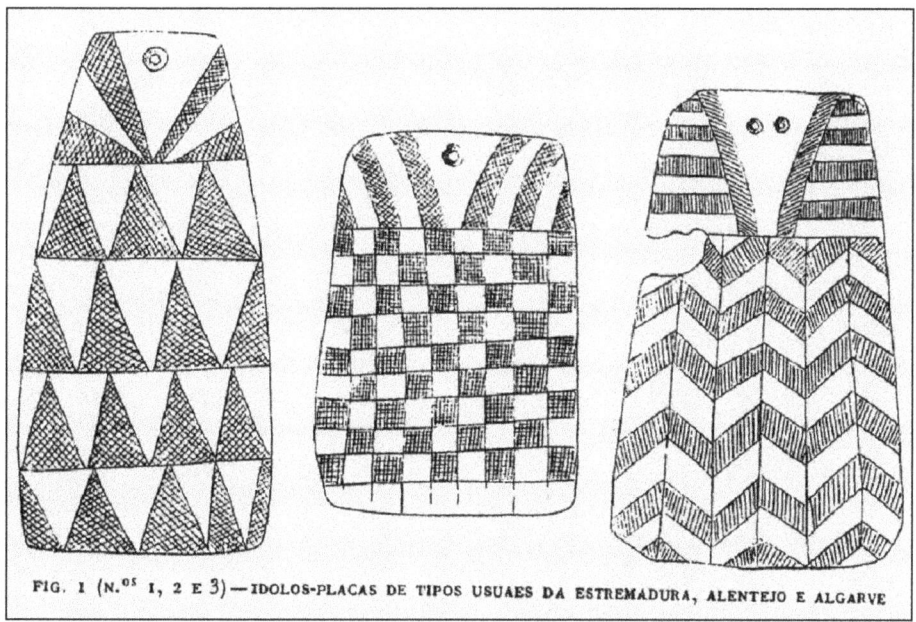

Fig. 6.4. Engraved plaques from dolmens excavated during the 19th century

set within a group of material characteristics – perfectly delimited in space and time – and for this reason it also captured the diffusionist and migrational contexts. In the words of the archaeologist and art historian, Professor Vergílio Correia Pinto da Fonseca (1888-1944), on the subject of certain rock paintings:

> "*The stylised and schematic character of those figures shows that they are Neolithic, similar to those discovered throughout the neighbouring country, especially in the mountains of the South, betraying the occupation of the Peninsula by a single population in race and culture*" (Correia, 1922, p. 147).

In fact this was a statement almost replicating Kossinna's theory of the symbiosis between a race and its material culture, at a time when the existence of engraved plaques was being reiterated and considered as specific to the megalithic culture of Portugal, even though its use and meaning were widely discussed.

CONCLUSION

Independently of these questions, the efforts of Portuguese scholars – many working in the context of activities developed in connection with the Royal Association of Portuguese Archaeologists – led to the creation, in 1881, of the Commission for National Monuments (*Commissão dos Monumentos Nacionaes*). The crowning glory of this work was the publication, in 1910, of the first list of sites classified as "national monuments", which included dolmens and standing stones (Fig. 6.5). This list, slightly different from the one compiled a few years earlier, was also the result of successive explorations conducted in the field by Professor José Leite de Vasconcellos (1858-1941), archa-

Fig. 6.5. Front page of the first inventory of ancient monuments published in 1881 by the Commission for National Monuments (Commissão dos Monumentos Nacionaes)

eologist and ethnographer as well as the mentor and director of the Portuguese Ethnographic Museum (*Museu Ethnographico Português*); he maintained a particular interest in this archaeological typology even though the location of so many of many of these monuments on private lands greatly complicated their effective preservation.

References

A.H./A.A.P. (1889) *Actas da Assembleia Geral*. Lisboa. 132, 7/4.

A.H./A.A.P. (1889) *Actas da Assembleia Geral*. Lisboa. 137, 22/12.

CORREIA, V. (1922) Arte rupestre em Portugal. A Pala Pinta. Aditamento. *Terra Portuguesa*, 32-34, p. 147.

CORREIA, V. (1873Discussion. *Compte Rendu de la 1ère session de l'Association Française pour l'Avancement des Sciences*. Paris: Secrétariat de l'Association, p. 726.

I.A.N./T.T. (1876a) – *Correspondência artistica e scientifica mantida com J. Possidónio da Silva*. Lisboa. VIIIa, 8.ª, 1260.

I.A.N./T.T. (1876b) – *Correspondência artistica e scientifica mantida com J. Possidónio da Silva*. Lisboa. VIIIa, 8.ª, 1353.

I.A.N./T.T. (1879) *Correspondência artistica e scientifica mantida com J. Possidónio da Silva*. Lisboa. XI, 8.ª, 1767.

I.A.N./T.T. (1885) *Correspondência artistica e scientifica mantida com J. Possidónio da Silva*. Lisboa. XVI, 8.ª, 3320.

MARTINS, A.C. (1999a) Introduction and Conclusion. *The Archaeology of Nationalism*: "*The Example of the Nineteenth Portuguese Archaeology*". *Abstracts Book of the 5th Annual Meeting of the European Association of Archaeologists*. Bournemouth.

MARTINS, A.C. (1999b) Possidónio da Silva, a *RAACAP* e os Estudos Pré-Históricos no Portugal Oitocentista. *Arqueologia*. Porto. 24.

MARTINS, A.C. (1999c) Possidónio da Silva, a *RAACAP*, e a Arqueologia no Portugal de Oitocentos. A Conservação dos Monumentos Arqueológicos. *Actas do 3º Congresso de Arqueologia Peninsular*. Vila Real.

MARTINS, A.C. (2001a) Estudos Pré-históricos e Nacionalismo: uma Perspectiva Possidoniana. *Revista Portuguesa de Arqueologia*. Lisboa. 4: 1.

MARTINS, A.C. (2001b) O 1.º *Curso Elementar de Archeologia* (Lisboa, 1885). *Trabalhos de Antropologia e Etnologia*. Porto. 55.

MARTINS, A.C. (2003) *Possidónio da Silva (1806-1896) e o Elogio da Memória. Um Percurso na Arqueologia de Oitocentos*. Lisboa: AAP.

MELLO, A.J. de (1886) Primeiro Curso de Archeologia. *Boletim de Architectura e Archeologia*. Lisboa. S. 2, 5: 9, p. 121.

SILVA, J.P.N. da (1897) Notice sur les Monuments Mégalithiques du Portugal. *Association Française pour l'Avancement des Sciences*. Paris: Secrétariat de l'Association.

SILVA, J.P.N. da (1881a) Archeologia Prehistorica. *Boletim de Architectura e Archeologia*. Lisboa. S. 2, 3: 5, p. 69-71.

SILVA, J.P.N. da (1881b) Fouilles faites dans les dolmens en Portugal, en 1881 *Compte Rendu de la 11ème session de l'Association Française pour l'Avancement des Sciences*. Paris: Secrétariat de l'Association, p. 620.

SILVA, J.P.N. da (1888a) Monumentos Celticos. *Boletim de Architectura e Archeologia*. Lisboa. S. 2, 6: 2, p. 26.

SILVA, J.P.N. da (1888b) Monumentos Celticos. *Boletim de Architectura e Archeologia*. Lisboa. S. 2, 6: 9, p. 7.

WILLIAM GREENWELL AND THE DIVERSITY OF ANTIQUARIANISM

Jeff SANDERS

Society of Antiquaries of Scotland, National Museums of Scotland, Chambers Street, Edinburgh

Abstract: When examining the work of those 19th century men and women with an interest in prehistory, it is easy to label them as 'antiquarian'. Their work is caught up in wider explanatory frameworks, such as Romantic nationalism, or seen as the primitive forerunner of more modern archaeological concerns with preservation, or the development of fieldwork techniques. This paper seeks to explore these issues in relation to the life and work of William Greenwell (1820-1918), a prodigious fieldworker and archaeological author. It is suggested that the broader themes used to characterise this period do not adequately address the variety of methodological and interpretative activities within the early archaeological community.
Keywords: *Greenwell, antiquarianism, Romanticism*

Résumé: Quand on examine le travail des gens du XIXe qui s'intéressaient à la Préhistoire, il est facile de les considérer comme des 'antiquaires'. En fait, leur travail s'insère dans une plus large structure explicative, telle que le Nationalisme romantique, ou est considéré comme le pionnier des questions archéologiques plus modernes sur la préservation ou sur le développement des techniques agricoles. Cet article tente d'examiner les problèmes liés à la vie et à l'oeuvre de William Greenwell (1820-1918), agriculteur exceptionnel et auteur archéologue. Nous pensons que les grands thèmes utilisés pour caractériser cette période ne reflètent pas la diversité des activités méthodologiques et interprétatives menées au sein de la communauté archéologique.
Mots clés: *Greenwell, antiquarianisme, Romantisme*

INTRODUCTION

Caricatures, such as the late 18th century illustration *Death and the Antiquaries* by Thomas Rowlandson (Fig. 7.1) depicting the opening of the tomb of King Edward I (Peltz & Myrone 1999, 2), highlight the reputation for stuffiness, unhealthy obsession with death and fetishism that antiquarian pursuits had acquired by that time. During the 19th century, the portrayal of moribund, barrow-digging gentleman-dilettantes still had influence, although it was combated with appeals to scientific rigour and an increasing acceptance of physical objects as suitable source material for information on the past (Momigliano 1950, Murray 1989, 64). Bruce Trigger reflects the continuation of this stereotype of antiquarians in modern accounts: "Romantically inclined individuals developed a strong interest in ruined abbeys, graves and other symbols of death and decay, including human skeletons grinning 'a ghastly smile'" (Trigger 2003, 66), and this remains an influential characterisation of antiquarian activity.

As with all caricatures, within these representations there is both an element of exaggeration and a grain of truth. When exploring the antiquarian background from which archaeology emerges, broad themes constantly recur. Nationalism, for example, is often viewed as the defining feature of much of the archaeological work undertaken in the late 18th and 19th centuries, with its ideological roots closely associated with the Romantic movement (Trigger 1995). However, the impact of Romantic thought reached much further, and influenced archaeology in many more nuanced ways than the simple conflation of Romanticism with Nationalism suggests. Nostalgia for a pre-industrial way of life, for example, provided one such area of Romantic influence, with the projection of an idealised rural and noble existence onto the past often being the result of this nostalgia, especially in the more heavily industrialised regions. Similarly, the concept of 'preservation' displayed a subtly different meaning during the 19th century than it does today, and belied a range of more complex processes at work (Sweet 2004, 303, Morgan Evans 2004, Hunter 1981). It becomes apparent, when examining the individual biographies of those working during the early development of archaeology, that the wider themes used to characterise groups of people do not adequately account for the diverse nature of antiquarianism. It is the purpose of this paper to address a few of the broad strokes used when exploring antiquarianism and to suggest that in a similar way to their portrayal in caricature, discussion of antiquarianism focuses on stereotypical characteristics within which much diversity is suppressed.

WILLIAM GREENWELL – BROAD THEMES

These issues can be explored through examination of the life and work of William Greenwell (1820-1918), who would probably have objected to being labelled a 'Romantic'. However, Greenwell fits the profile of a 19th century dilettante perfectly (Levine 1986, 6) – he had a wide range of interests, from prehistoric archaeology to numismatics. After a university education at Durham he was ordained as an Anglican minister and became a minor canon and librarian in the same city. With confidence, due to his education, occupation and interests, Greenwell can be labelled as 'middle class'. The close association of archaeology and bourgeois interests made excavation, collection and survey socially acceptable pursuits (Trigger 2003, 117). Greenwell's profession afforded him the time to undertake his archaeological work and actively encouraged his interest in the preservation of ecclesiastical architecture (Levine 1986 48).

Fig. 7.1. "Death and the Antiquary", early 19th century satirical caricature by Thomas Rowlandson depicting antiquaries on the occasion of the opening of the tomb of King Edward I in Westminster Abbey

When examining his life's work it is easy to portray Greenwell as working within a conservative and nationalist tradition. His main work, *British Barrows*, published in 1877, contains a number of references to a specifically *English* past, tracing the particulars of the *English* character and conflating 'Britishness' with 'Englishness';

> *"Our own English ancestors might, no doubt, have been understood by us in many of their great characteristics, in their obedience to law, their love of justice and of freedom, and their aptitude for self-government, for these by an unswerving tradition have passed down, by slow gradations of change, unto ourselves"* (Greenwell 1877, 58).

The portrayal of British (specifically English) ancestors in a benign light was part of a much earlier tradition. The work of the antiquarian William Stukeley (1687-1765) is a notable example of romantically-themed description of pre-Roman culture (Piggott 1985). Illustrations of prehistoric Britons, heavily influenced by depictions of indigenous North American and Pacific communities, contributed to the invention of a noble and ancient people (Pratt 2005). An example of a suitably 'noble' prehistoric ancestor is provided by S.R. Meyrick and C.H. Smith's "An Arch Druid in his Judicial Habit" (Fig. 7.2), the illustration emphasising both the civilised nature of British prehistory, and the wilder excesses of Romantic imagination (Piggott 1968, 226).

Initially, this appears to fit perfectly with Greenwell's chauvinistically-imagined English ancestor. However, the nationalist theme fails to account for a more nuanced set of influences. Greenwell's own preoccupations seem much more at a regional, rather than national, level. Greenwell's native Northumbria, for example, exerted a coherent local identity based upon a shared sense of a Saxon past (Sweet 2004, chapter 6), which is lost in generalised accounts of 'nationalism'. This is likely to have affected Greenwell, who went on to carry out most of his archaeological work in Yorkshire, a county with a strong regional identity and history of antiquarian investigation (Marsden 1974, 90). The importance of local history is reflected in the number of antiquaries confining the majority of their work to one county, such as the Reverend J.C. Atkinson (1814-1900) and J.R. Mortimer (1825-1911) in Yorkshire, or W.C. Borlase (1848-1899) in Cornwall. The genre of county history was a popular choice of antiquarian publication, exemplified by Sir Richard Colt Hoare's *Ancient Wiltshire* (Morse 1999, 8), which strongly influenced Greenwell's own work.

Additionally, the antiquarian community of which Greenwell was an active participant was international in both outlook and membership. Greenwell was in contact with many antiquarians, both at home and abroad, and the records of their meetings, for example the *International Congress of Prehistoric Archaeology* (1869), do not

Fig. 7.2. "An Arch Druid in His Judicial Habit": an illustration from S.R. Meyrick and C.H. Smith publication of 1815 *The Costume of the Original Inhabitants of the British Isles*

display overtly chauvinistic overtones. The close-knit nature of the antiquarian community also led to the diffusion of explanatory models from those working in other countries into the work of British antiquarians. Sven Nilsson's comparison of houses to tombs, for example (1868), suggesting a 'house for the dead', was absorbed into many antiquarian accounts, including Greenwell's discussion of barrow burial (1877, 2-3).

The issue of 'preservation' is also more complex than it may at first appear. An increasing concern with the preservation of monuments can be identified as evolving from the late 18th to the end of the 19th centuries, closely associated with both nationalism and increasing public awareness of prehistory (Sweet 2004, chapter 8, Murray 1989, 59). However, attitudes toward preservation among the antiquarian community in the 19th century diverged in several respects from more recent viewpoints. Greenwell, as an avid collector, carried out excavation for two purposes that seem at odds with a modern perspective. On the one hand, he published his findings, shared information and helped to reveal more about the prehistoric past. On the other, sites were selected that were likely to provide a good source of artefacts. It is revealing that *British Barrows* contains no archaeological plans or sections, but features instead a series of detailed

Fig. 7.3. An "urn" from the Kilmartin Glebe cairn included in Greenwell's 1877 publication "British Barrows"

illustrations of notable pottery or stone tools such as the 'urn' from Kilmartin glebe (Fig. 7.3). This reveals what Greenwell deemed worthy to be saved, and he was accused of occasionally omitting barrows with no impressive finds from his accounts due to his collector's instinct: "As with most antiquaries, Greenwell's interest in excavation seems to have derived from his role as a collector. He accumulated antiquities throughout his life in a determined and, occasionally, unprincipled fashion" (Kinnes & Longworth 1985, 10). In this respect however, Greenwell was not significantly different from most of his contemporaries.

So far, the less palatable side of antiquarian investigation has been highlighted, although this does Greenwell a disservice. He was an active campaigner for preservation, particularly through his activities as a member of the Society for the Protection of Ancient Buildings and as founder of the Archaeological and Architectural Society of Durham and Northumberland. He was also instrumental in the formation of a committee charged with the preservation of megalithic monuments, set up in response to the treatment of megaliths in Brittany (International Congress of Prehistoric Archaeology 1869, 417). For all his collector's instincts, Greenwell believed in the instructive value of artefacts and catalogued his own collection (Kinnes & Longworth 1985, 10). This belief in the potential of artefacts to educate was coupled with Greenwell's vision of them as providing a suitable base upon which to build theory in an inductive manner: "We need to heap flint on flint, to add bronze to bronze, in order that the base of our theory may be laid upon the firm substructure of well-sifted and oft-recurring detail" (Greenwell 1865, 98). The focus on objects, both as part of a collection and as the principle building block of scientific reconstruction of the past, helps explain the concentration on the representation of finds, rather than plans or sections, in Greenwell's work. Within antiquarian circles, the formation of county archaeological societies provided a forum for the sharing of material alongside the construction of county histories and museum collections (Levine 1986, 54).

In terms of the wider socio-political climate, the rights of the landowner were seen as sacrosanct during Greenwell's time, although they were being gradually eroded (Cannadine 1996). This in part explains the objections aroused whenever an attempt was made to pass an Ancient Monuments Act (Murray 1989, 62). The importance of preservation today owes much to the public appreciation of the past (Fowler 1981, Hunter 1981). In Greenwell's time this was just beginning to manifest itself, as prehistoric remains were in the process of being opened up to the public – both physically, in terms of access through the countryside (Bowden 1991, 149, Piggott 1976, 122), and conceptually, in terms of the realisation of the considerable time depth of prehistory (Daniels 1962).

Identification of the diverse influences contained within the concepts of 'nationalism' and 'preservation' is perhaps conditioned by a modern perspective that can view the subsequent development of archaeology from the 19th century into the culture history of the 20th century. Greenwell's contribution to the early development of archaeology before these 'paradigms' were identified is important, and it is difficult to identify him retrospectively as either 'antiquarian' or 'early archaeologist'.

GREENWELL'S CONTRIBUTION

It could be considered unfair to attempt to judge Greenwell's contribution in relation to modern standards. His major work falls into the period when archaeology was establishing itself as a credible scientific discipline – for W. Chapman, the years 1860 to 1870 see archaeology developing from an 'essentially dilettantist avocation' to 'an organised discipline' (1989, 34). Greenwell's work played an important role in the ultimate acceptance of the Three Age System in England (e.g. 1865, 255-8; 1877, 58), alongside the work of contemporaries such as John Lubbock's *Pre-historic Times* (1865) or Daniel Wilson's *The Archaeology and Prehistoric Annals of Scotland* (1851). Although Greenwell refers to the scheme as "*Denmark's* stone, bronze, and iron ages" (1877, 58; my emphasis), his initial worries concerning the theory seem to have been based not on the idea, but on the present state of archaeological knowledge (*ibid*, 130-2). Similarly, a number of the archaeological concepts in use today – such as the term 'Neolithic' – owe much to their definition and popularisation by authors such as Greenwell (e.g. 1877, 131). This can be viewed in relation to the acceptance of an increasingly ancient prehistory, although Greenwell and his contemporaries could not fully appreciate the considerable antiquity of many of the barrows they excavated. Generally, the barrows were attributed to a pre-Roman period, with only general speculation as to how much older they could be (e.g. Greenwell 1865, 255, 1877, 131).

Certain aspects of Greenwell's fieldwork certainly fit the term 'antiquarian'. His field methodology, where apparent, was more geared to the swift extraction of artefacts than to gathering maximum information about the past;

> "My practice has always been to drive a trench, the width of the barrow as it was originally constituted and before it was enlarged by being ploughed down, from South to North, through and beyond the centre. I have not always found it necessary to remove the whole of the North and West sides, as they are generally found to be destitute of secondary interments; in very many cases, however, I have turned over the whole mound" (Greenwell 1877, 27).

This field methodology fits into a wider tradition of barrow-opening aimed at quickly recovering the primary burial and any associated finds (Marsden 1974, 99). Barrow-opening could also draw crowds of interested onlookers alongside the workmen and volunteers under the supervision of the antiquarian (Marsden 1974, 30-1).

Re-examination of several of Greenwell's excavations has revealed occasional discrepancies in recording detail alongside more serious omissions. Rival barrow-opener John Mortimer and his brother Robert criticised Greenwell over his excavation technique, specifically his occasional lack of supervision and disinterest in barrows containing no finds (Marsden 1974, 100-104). At the long mound at Willerby it has been suggested that Greenwell did not fully excavate a cremation deposit, and that he did not always excavate down to the pre-barrow surface (Manby 1963, 175). Greenwell also seems to have missed burials and other features at several sites such as at Weaverthorpe, Cowlam and Folkton (Kinnes & Longworth 1985, 13). In common with other barrow-diggers, the relatively small excavation areas used by Greenwell probably contributed to the failure to uncover all of the features and artefacts, and large areas of the covering mound of several monuments were left unexcavated (Manby 1963, 195).

Compared to many of his contemporaries, however, Greenwell's excavation techniques were superior and he kept good records of his collections and activities, publishing promptly. He investigated a large number of sites, predominantly in the north of England, and published several of them (e.g. Greenwell 1865, 1866, 1870, 1877, 1881). His main written work was undoubtedly *British Barrows* (1877), although he continued to excavate and write for many years afterwards. The key model for *British Barrows*, and many other antiquarian accounts of prehistory, was Sir Richard Colt Hoare's *Ancient Wiltshire*, published between 1810 to 1812 and frequently referred to by Greenwell (e.g. 1877, 14, note 1). Stuart Piggott has lamented the fact that little appeared to have changed between Colt Hoare's time and that of Greenwell (1989, 157-8). This is unfair, however, and although Greenwell is an obvious admirer of Colt Hoare's work, he provides a critique – however tactfully veiled – where appropriate (e.g. Greenwell 1877, 25 note 3). In turn, Greenwell's rival, J.R. Mortimer, used the introduction to *British Barrows* as a model for his own book – *Forty Years' Researches in British and Saxon Burial Mounds of East Yorkshire* (Mortimer 1905, Kinnes & Longworth 1985, 13). Greenwell also broke somewhat from the stereotype of the barrow-digger by investigating the quarry site of Grime's Graves (1870), proving it was a flint mine through excavation, establishing a sequence of construction and dating it to the Neolithic based on artefactual evidence. In contrast to his later work, Greenwell's account of Grime's Graves also contains a plan (1870, 424; Fig. 7.4) indicating an interest stretching further than the simple recovery and discussion of artefacts.

Greenwell also eschews the characterisation of antiquarianism as simply an inductive pursuit through the considerable thought he gives to the variety of symbolic and ritual roles that material culture might represent. This is at odds with his stated aims of speaking from facts and not theories (Greenwell 1865, 98). In *British Barrows* he speculates on a variety of themes, ranging from what people wore to the significance of fire (1877, 30, 32). Tim Murray has suggested that the identification of antiquarianism with the inductive method is connected to attempts on the part of prehistorians to cement credibility by linking their methodology to the dominant scientific approach (1989, 59). This would appear a reasonable explanation for the dichotomy between Greenwell's stated method and its actual realisation in *British Barrows*. Greenwell's work appears dated in terms of the explanatory models he uses; his education continually resurfaces in the selection of analogy in order to explain his findings, and a reference to *Hamlet* even appears in *British Barrows* (1877, 11). Similarly a form of primitivism, or search for origins, arises in his descriptions of prehistoric people and places as ancient antecedents of current political or religious institutions (e.g. Greenwell 1877, 58; 1866, 337). This was very much a popular mode of explanation at the time, and sat very well with the ideas of evolutionary sequences which were thought illustrative of human 'progress' (Gosden 1999, 62-3; Trigger 2003, chapter 3). The role of ancestors was also an important explanatory model for Greenwell – particularly the noble predecessors of the English (1877, 58) – and can again be connected to the search for origins, in this particular example, of a people. A tension can also be identified, however, between the concept of human 'progress' and the contemporary concern of the preservation of a rural idyll in the face of increasing industrialisation (Levine 1986, 52; Piggott 1976) – a major Romantic theme.

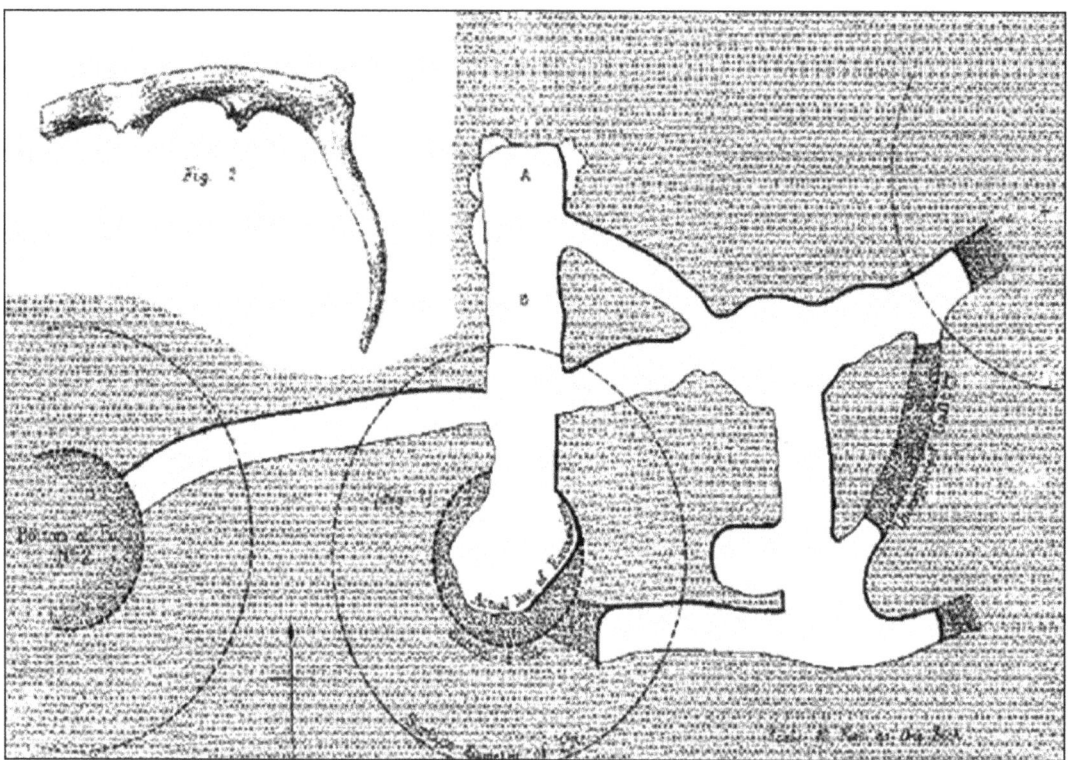

Fig. 7.4. Greenwell's plan of Grime's Graves quarry site (Greenwell 1870)

Another aspect of Romantic influence was the connection between particularising and historicist accounts of nationalism and racial theories. A good example of this translated into archaeology was the popularity of craniology. In this area, Greenwell was obviously influenced by the work of John Thurnam (1864), and the co-author of *British Barrows*, George Rolleston (1876). The physical dimensions of the skull were considered to have a direct bearing on the racial characteristics of the individual. Evidence based on these assumptions was then considered methodologically secure enough to apply to prehistoric evidence and used to indicate the movement of people. Using prehistoric remains in this way, the past was manipulated to provide evidence of the progressive trajectory history would take until reaching its pinnacle in modern Europe. In its British incarnation, and that adopted by Greenwell as a refinement of Thurnam's approach, this is portrayed as a series of invaders whose superior qualities were amalgamated with those of the locals (1877, 127-9). In its archaeological application, craniology was also regarded as scientifically sound enough to provide a form of secure dating evidence (Morse 1999), and this is cautiously accepted by Greenwell in *British Barrows*.

CONCLUSIONS

In conclusion, the life and work of William Greenwell acts as a reminder of how individuals working within an antiquarian tradition diverged from the broad explanatory models used to characterise the period as a whole. In terms of nationalist discourse and preservation, explanations that at face value appear straightforward belie an underlying complexity. In these terms the nationalist impact, particularly in terms of Romantic thought, may be overplayed in modern accounts and can obscure other factors at work, such as regionalism or the ongoing tension between the 'rural idyll' and the forces of industrialisation. Similarly, the idea of antiquarians as using a purely inductive approach also masks the underlying presence of analogy within evolutionary accounts (Wylie 2002, 137-141). Primitivism, for example, was clearly a deductive principle applied before more inductive approaches. A range of ethnographic data was also being employed, alongside ever popular classical analogies. Several of the explanatory models in use today, such as the idea of monumental tombs as 'houses for the dead' (Nilsson 1868), first found coherent voice in the 19th century. When examining the work of those 19th century men and women with an interest in the prehistoric remains around them, it is hard not to label them as either 'antiquarians' or 'early archaeologists'. However, the work of William Greenwell illustrates that these terms themselves do not cover the wide variety of methodological and interpretative activities undertaken by a number of different people at this time.

References

BOWDEN, M. (1991) *Pitt Rivers*. Cambridge: Cambridge University Press.

CANNADINE, D. (1996) *The Decline and Fall of the British Aristocracy*. London: Papermac.

CHAPMAN, W. (1989) The Organisational Context in the History of Archaeology: Pitt-Rivers and Other British Archaeologists in the 1860's. *The Antiquaries Journal,* Vol. LXIX, p. 23-42.

DANIEL, G. (1962) *The Idea of Prehistory*. London: C.A. Watts & Co.

Fowler, P.J. (1981) Archaeology, the Public and the Sense of the Past. In Lowenthal, D. & Binney, M. (eds.) *Our Past before Us: Why do We Save It?* London: Temple Smith, p. 56-69.

GOSDEN, C. (1999) *Anthropology and Archaeology: A Changing Relationship*. London: Routledge.

GREENWELL, W.G. (1865) Notices of the Examinations of Ancient Grave-hills in the North Riding of Yorkshire. *Archaeological Journal* 22, p. 97-117, and 241-263.

GREENWELL, W.G. (1866) An Account of Excavations in Cairns near Crinan. *Proceedings of the Society of Antiquaries of Scotland* 6, p. 336-51.

GREENWELL, W.G. (1870) On the Opening of Grime's Graves in Norfolk. *The Journal of the Ethnological Society of London*, vol. 2: 4, p. 419-439.

GREENWELL, W.G. (1877) *British Barrows*. Oxford: Clarendon Press.

GREENWELL, W.G. (1881) On Barrows at Aldbourne, Wiltshire, and their Contents. *Proceedings of the Society of Antiquaries of London* 8, p. 175-179.

HUNTER, M. (1981) The Preconditions of Preservation: A Historical Perspective. In: Lowenthal, D. & Binney, M. (eds.) *Our Past before Us: Why do We Save It?* London: Temple Smith, p. 22-32.

INTERNATIONAL CONGRESS OF PREHISTORIC ARCHAEOLOGY (1869) *Transactions of the Third Session Which Opened at Norwich on the 20th August and Closed in London on the 28th August 1868*. London: Longmans, Green and Co.

KINNES, I & LONGWORTH, I.H. (1985) *Catalogue of the Excavated Prehistoric and Romano-British Material in the Greenwell Collection*. London: British Museum Publications.

LEVINE, P. (1986) *The Amateur and the Professional*. Cambridge: Cambridge University Press.

LUBBOCK, J. (1865) *Pre-historic Times, as Illustrated by Ancient Remains, and the Manners and Customs of Modern Savages*. London: Longmans, Green.

MANBY, T.G. (1963) The Excavation of the Willerby Wold Long Barrow, East Riding of Yorkshire. *Proceedings of the Prehistoric Society* 29, p. 173-205.

MARSDEN, B.M. (1974) *The Early Barrow-Diggers*. Aylesbury: Shire Publications.

MOMIGLIANO, A. (1950) Ancient History and the Antiquarian. *Journal of the Warburg and Courtauld Institutes* 13, p. 285-315.

MORGAN EVANS, D. (2004) Et in Arcadia? The Problems with Ruins. *The Antiquaries Journal* 84, p. 411-422.

MORSE, M. (1999) Craniology and the Adoption of the Three-Age System in Britain. *Proceedings of the Prehistoric Society* 65, p. 1-16.

MORTIMER, J.R. (1905) *Forty Years' Researches in British and Saxon Burial Mounds of East Yorkshire: Including Romano-British Discoveries, and a Description of the Ancient Entrenchments on a Section of the Yorkshire Wolds*. London: A. Brown.

MURRAY, T. (1989) The History, Philosophy and Sociology of Archaeology: the Case of the Ancient Monuments Protection Act (1882). In: Pinsky, V. & Wylie, A (eds.) *Critical Traditions in Contemporary Archaeology*. Albuquerque: University of New Mexico Press, p. 55-67.

NILSSON, S. (1868) *The Primitive Inhabitants of Scandinavia: An Essay on Comparative Ethnography, and a Contribution to the History of the Development of Mankind*. 3rd Edition. London: Longmans, Green.

PELTZ, L. & MYRONE, M. (1999) 'Mine are the Subjects Rejected by the Historian': Antiquarianism, History and the Making of Modern Culture. In: Myrone, M. & Peltz, L. (eds.) *Producing the Past: Aspects of Antiquarian Culture and Practice 1700-1850*. Aldershot: Ashgate, p. 1-13.

PIGGOTT, S. (1968) *The Druids*. London: Thames & Hudson.

PIGGOTT, S. (1976) *Ruins in a Landscape: Essays in Antiquarianism*. Edinburgh: Edinburgh University Press.

PIGGOTT, S. (1985) *William Stukeley: An Eighteenth-Century Antiquary*. London: Thames & Hudson.

PIGGOTT, S. (1989) *Ancient Britons and the Antiquarian Imagination: Ideas from the Renaissance to the Regency*. London: Thames & Hudson.

PRATT, S. (2005) The American Time Machine: Indians and the Visualization of Ancient Europe. In: Smiles, S. & Moser, S. (eds.) *Envisioning the Past: Archaeology and the Image*, Malden MA: Blackwell, p. 51-71.

ROLLESTON, G. (1876) On the People of the Long Barrow Period. *Journal of the Anthropological Institute* 5, p. 120-173.

SWEET, R. (2004) *Antiquaries*. London: Hambledon and London.

THURNAM, J. (1864) On the Two Principal Forms of Ancient British and Gaulish Skulls. *Memoirs of the Anthropological Society* 1, p. 120-168.

TRIGGER, B. (1995) Romanticism, Nationalism, and Archaeology. In: Kohl, P. & Fawcett, C. (eds.) *Nationalism, Politics, and the Practice of Archaeology,* Cambridge: Cambridge University Press, p. 263-279.

TRIGGER, B. (2003) *A History of Archaeological Thought.* Cambridge: Cambridge University Press.

WILSON, D. (1851) *The Archaeology and Prehistoric Annals of Scotland.* Edinburgh: Sutherland and Knox.

WYLIE, A. (2002) *Thinking from Things: Essays in the Philosophy of Archaeology.* London: University of California Press.

THE LUKIS FAMILY OF GUERNSEY AND THE STUDY OF MEGALITHS IN THE 19TH CENTURY

Heather SEBIRE

Guernsey Museum

Abstract: *Fredrick Corbin Lukis (1788-1871) F.S.A, antiquarian and natural historian, was born and lived all his life in St Peter Port, Guernsey. As a young man he became interested in a wide variety of disciplines including natural history, botany, geology, conchology and science but it was archaeology, and in particular megaliths, that held his attention throughout most of his life. He was elected a Fellow of the Society of Antiquaries in 1853, and communicated many letters to the Secretary and other Members. Four of Lukis' children became archaeologists in their own right, all contributing in their own way to megalithic studies. This paper summarises the contribution of the Lukis family to megalithic studies in the nineteenth century.*
Key words: Megaliths, Lukis, Guernsey, antiquarian

Résumé: *Fredrick Corbin Lukis (1788-1871) F.S.A, antiquaire et naturaliste, naquit et vécut toute sa vie à St Peter Port, Guernesey. Jeune homme, il développa un intérêt pour une grande variété de disciplines, comprenant l'histoire naturelle, la botanique, la géologie, la conchologie et la science mais ce fut l'archéologie, et en particulier les mégalithes, qui tinrent son attention pendant pratiquement toute sa vie. Il fut élu comme membre de la Société des Antiquaires en 1853, et communiqua de nombreuses lettres au secrétaire et aux autres membres.*
Quatre des enfants de Lukis devinrent eux-mêmes archéologues, et contribuèrent tous de leur façon à l'étude des mégalithes. Cet article résume la contribution de la famille Lukis à l'étude des mégalithes au 19ème siècle.
Mots-clés: *Mégalithes, Lukis, Guernesey, antiquaire*

FREDERICK CORBIN LUKIS F.S.A.

Archaeology

Lukis Senior tells us in his own words that his interest in 'the prehistoric remains of his native island' was first awakened in 1809, when he started to examine carefully the various sites of Guernsey's 'druidical altars', as the megalithic tombs were called at that time (Lukis 1848, V, 21). He first visited the site at Le Déhus in 1809, most probably in the company of Joshua Gosselin, who himself sketched and made notes on the structure of the monument, from the outset using the language of the observer. Two years later, in 1811, his interest in these ancient monuments was increased. This was due to his part in the discovery of the passage grave of La Varde, at L'Ancresse in the Vale parish. Frederick, by then a young man of twenty-three years, was taken, again by Joshua Gosselin, to examine a new find on L'Ancresse Common. The tomb had been exposed some years previously in 1793 by soldiers while they were digging entrenchments on the top of the hill. Fortunately, the excavation of the interior was abandoned for fear of the structure collapsing. The sand drifting into the chamber, after the soldiers had abandoned their work in 1793, had soon covered the remains and preserved them from further damage. So years later, in 1811, when soldiers under the orders of General Doyle were building a redoubt, they thought they had discovered an artificial cavern.

They were digging through pottery and bones when Gosselin and Lukis arrived on the scene. Lukis movingly describes the effect seeing the tomb had on him (Lukis *ibid*.):

"The sight of this singular structure, emerging – after the lapse of many centuries – from the hill on which it stands and protruding, as it were, for the first time since its construction, from the ground which covered it, made a deep impression on the writer's mind."

We are not told whether this visit happened because they had heard of the discovery, or whether it was just by coincidence that Gosselin had decided to visit the spot on that particular day. However, Lukis tells us that after examining the tomb he and Gosselin went away, each with a human skull under their arm (Lukis 1848, V, 7).

Early investigations in Guernsey

Lukis tried at the time to form a society of interested parties in order to undertake the excavation of the tomb but, owing to the lack of interest in archaeology, he met with no success. This must have been frustrating for a young man so full of enthusiasm for his newly discovered interest. Gosselin was so enthused by the discovery that he wrote a letter to Sir Joseph Banks describing the find. The letter was read to the Society of Antiquaries in London on 5th December 1811 and was published in *Archaeologia* two years later (Gosselin 1813).

It was some years later however, in the late 1830s, that Lukis carried out his greatest amount of archaeological excavation and recording, particularly on the megaliths of his native home. He recorded that in 1837 he 'determined to begin the excavation of the prehistoric remains of the Channel Islands' (Lukis 1848, V, 30). He began by returning to the great 'dolmen' of La Varde at L'Ancresse in August 1837, and by the end of December that year he

Fig. 8.1. Lukis recording excavations at Le Creux des Fées, Guernsey, in 1840 © Guernsey Museum and Art Gallery

had thoroughly examined no less than four other 'dolmens': Le Tombeau du Grand Sarrazin, La Roche qui Sonne, Le Trépied and La Mare ès Mauves, and a portion of the great 'dolmen' of Le Déhus.

The island of Herm, which lies to the east of Guernsey directly opposite St Peter Port, was visited during the year 1839 and Lukis and family marked 'six or seven spots during our walk over the island'. In 1842 Lukis went over to Herm again and spent some weeks excavating other 'dolmens' and cists and continued this work in 1844 and again in 1845. In 1840, back on Guernsey itself, he had excavated the 'dolmens' of La Platte Mare, L'Ancresse and La Creux des Fées and St Peter in the Wood. Lukis records that La Creux des Fées was the third largest on the island and still almost entirely covered with its mound. Also in 1844 he continued his work of excavating the Déhus, but it was not until 1847 that he was able to complete the work at this particular site.

Archaeological Excavations in England

Lukis excavated not only in Guernsey. In 1842, an examination of barrows on Bircham Heath in Norfolk was begun. This work grew out of a friendship with the Rolfe family in Norfolk, and many letters between Neville Rolfe and Frederick Lukis survive in the archive. Both Lukis' sons, William and John, had visited Heacham Hall, the family seat, during William's time at Cambridge. At Mr Rolfe's, John had read *Archaeologia*, 'a very voluminous work on antiquities', which he recommended to his father. In it he found a reference to the 'Druidical temple' from Jersey, which has been transported to the Conway estate near Henley-on-Thames. A short report of the archaeological work carried out on the Barrows was published as a pamphlet in Guernsey (Lukis 1843). In the introduction Lukis writes:

> *"The ignorance which prevails throughout the land, particularly amongst the labouring classes, on the nature of these memorials of an ancient race, has tended much to their partial removal or entire destruction"* (*ibid.*, 10).

He assumed the status of an authority on the subject and continued to bemoan the fact that the real purpose of the barrows was misinterpreted by many and the subject of 'marvellous stories'. He goes on to describe barrows which 'may be regarded as one of the earliest modes of burial', and compares them to Homer's description in the Iliad. He discusses the barrows of Wiltshire and Derbyshire and then the magnitude of Silbury Hill and Bartlow Hills in Cambridgeshire. In his notes he mentions Colt Hoare's 'Ancient Wiltshire', implying that he was familiar with the work.

He then goes into the detail of the work. One barrow had a shaft dug into it 'till the natural soil was perceptible', but had been disturbed and only yielded 'one small fragment of earthen vessel'. At the end of the short report Lukis even offers advice for the conservation of the finds (*ibid.* 14):

> *"It may be remarked here that glue or size, ought to be applied to all substances taken from ancient remains. Sun-baked vessels are thereby prevented from disintergrating, glazed vessels also from scaling and 'Terra Cotta' retains the red varnish without cracking."*

Although this is a relatively short publication it gives an insight into Lukis' methods and interpretation, and shows that he was interested in sites outside his own island.

THE LUKIS FAMILY

Frederick Corbin Lukis in fact created an archaeological dynasty. Many members of the family followed in their father's footsteps and became archaeologists in their own right, although the focus of their studies was more widespread. Frederick Collings, Lukis' eldest son, who became a doctor of medicine, helped his father excavate the Guernsey megaliths and he himself published a paper in *Archaeologia* (Lukis 1853), in which he summarised the megaliths in the Channel Islands and elsewhere, in a paper entitled 'Observations on the Celtic Megaliths'. This paper was based on three lectures delivered to the Society of Antiquaries at the special request of the members. He actually became a Fellow of the Society of Antiquaries before his father in 1853. He began his treatise by saying that:

> *"It is much regretted that of late years many individuals tempted by an unprofitable cupidity or an ignorant curiosity , have frequently assisted in the destruction of the little that had escaped the general wreck, which otherwise had proved of immense interest to the archaeologist: we may add to these the annihilating sway of modern agricultural and engineering operation" (ibid., 232).*

In the paper he bemoaned the fact that not enough attention had been paid to these 'structural remains attributed to the Celtic people'. He compared about forty sites from the Channel Islands with some in England and in France and was struck by the similarities, which he considered might suggest a 'definite architectural law' governing their construction. He bemoans the use of the term 'Druid's Altar' in reference to megalithic tombs, since its 'utter inapplicability to sacrificial purposes' was obvious. He goes on to categorise megaliths using the terms *maenhir*, *demi-dolmen*, *dolmen*, *cist-vaen*, *cromlech* and *peristalith*, and in his text he observes that Stonehenge must in fact have been built in two periods.

To accompany the text Frederick Junior had drawn up a table of 'Celtic Megaliths' which he set before the Society and which is reproduced in the *Collectanea Antiqua*. He continued with a detailed description of the various types, referring to well known sites outside Guernsey such as Avebury and Stonehenge. This work must have been carried out in collaboration with his father who had excavated the Guernsey 'cromlechs'.

Lukis' second son, John Walter, contributed to Captain Oliver's report on the Monuments of the Channel Islands which had been commissioned by the Society of Antiquaries of London (Oliver 1870), but the main bulk of his work was in France, where he conducted many excavations in the Côtes-du-Nord and Finistère regions. He was Vice President of the Société Scientifique de Morlaix from 1879 until his death in 1894. He published two papers relevant to Channel Islands archaeology in the Bulletin of the Société d'Etudes Scientifiques du Finistère: 'Note sur les anciens habitants et les monuments préhistoriques des Îles de Guernsey, Jersey, Aurigny etc.' (Lukis 1886) and 'Objets préhistoriques recueilles dans les monuments mégalithiques des Iles de Jersey, Guernsey, etc.' (Lukis 1888).

Excavation and Recording in Brittany

In his article 'Observations on the Primeaval Antiquities of the Channel Islands' (Lukis 1844), Lukis Senior had alluded to 'the celebrated cromlech in the isle of Gavr'Innis in the Morbihan'. The family had spent summer holidays in Brittany and the 'Accounts of various journies in the South of Brittany by John W.Lukis , Francis Du Bois Lukis, William C. Lukis myself and Mam' are written up in volume V of his *Collectanea Antiqua*.

There is a very detailed description of the monument on the Isle of Gavr'Innis by John, who wrote back to the family in the Grange from Vannes on May 3rd 1844 (Lukis 1848, V, 266). From the descriptions following John's letter, it is clear that F.C. Lukis himself visited the Isle of Gavr'Innis and many of the other monuments of Southern Brittany, but it is from John's visit that he seems to have become familiar with the carvings in the interior of the tomb.

Interestingly it was John's enthusiasm and his father's deductions that led them into a debate in London about the now famous carvings in the interior of the tomb at Gavr'Innis. In the Lukis correspondence there is a letter from Frederick Lukis to Charles Roach Smith, Secretary of the British Archaeological Association in 1848. This is a reply to a letter from Roach Smith in which he wrote to query the Messrs Lukis (i.e. John and his father) about the authenticity of the carvings on the props at Gavr'Innis as several members had 'declared publicly that Messrs Lukis were quite mistaken on the Artificial Character of the grooves and designs observed on the interior surfaces of props of Gavr'Innis and other cromlechs in the Morbihan'. John had published a paper entitled 'Gavr'Innis' in the Journal of the British Archaeological Association in

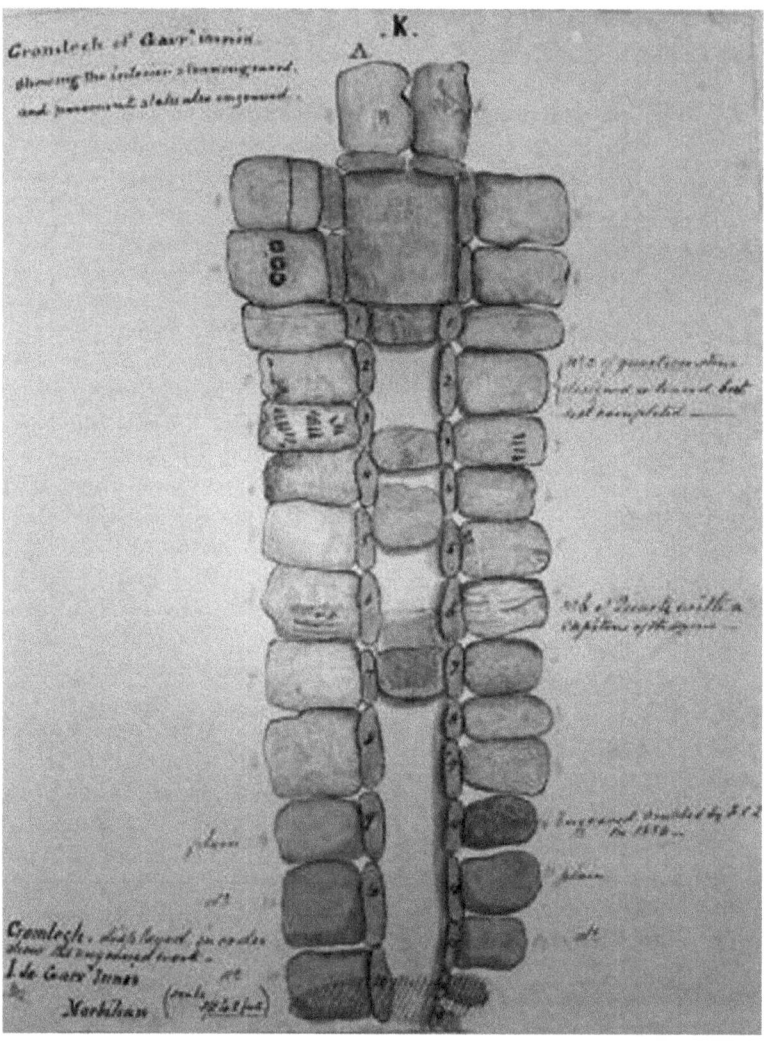

Fig. 8.2. Drawing of the carvings on the interior props at Gavr'Innis, Morbihan by J.W. Lukis © Guernsey Museum and Art Gallery

January 1848, in which he published a plan of the tomb and line drawings of the carvings on the props in the tomb at Gavr'Innis and also at Dol au Marchand. John compared them with ones he had heard about at New Grange in Ireland and a grave opened in Zealand, Denmark by Mr Hansen. Because of his knowledge of geology, Frederick Lukis was able to give an erudite explanation in his reply of 7th February 1848 to Roach Smith. Lukis pointed out that the local stone on Quiberon is granite and would not weather in such a uniform manner as the marks on the stones; after a long explanation of the properties of the rock he exhorted those who doubted to pay a visit to the site to see for themselves, after which he was sure that no one would doubt its authenticity.

The 'dispute' was written up in the London Literary Gazette of March 4th 1848. The article describes how Mr Smith had 'laid upon the table sketches of engraved stones in a cromlech in a plain in the bay of Morbihan in Brittany, published by the Society of Antiquaries of France and read in a paper by Mr F.C. Lukis, written in consequence of enquiries made at a preceding meeting. The article goes on to report Lukis' explanation of the geology, after which Smith stated 'that in his opinion the correct geological deductions they had been favoured with from their learned associate were perfectly conclusive'. He continued: 'Mr Lukis who unites the study of archaeology with an excellent knowledge of geology had demonstrated most clearly that no natural action of the primitive rocks by decomposition of any part or otherwise could by any possibility produce such regular depressions in the stones'. So it was through Frederick Lukis and his son John that the carvings on the props at Gavr'Innis were accepted as man-made by members of the British Archaeological Association. Lukis visited other sites in Brittany in the years around 1844. The Ile Longue cromlech, Dol ar Marchand, the cromlechs of Locmariaker and the great menhirs at Carnac were just some of the sites that received attention. Sketches of many of these in Lukis' own hand are included in the *Collectanea Antiqua* and are a forerunner to the wealth of more detailed plans that were executed by William Lukis and his friend Henry Dryden in the 1860s.

WILLIAM COLLINGS LUKIS

Particular mention must again be made of William Collings, Lukis' third son. Marsden, in his survey of the Barrow diggers, called him a scholar of European fame (1999, 79). He became the Reverend William Collings Lukis, M.A., F.S.A., and was the best known of the family for his archaeological work, especially in England. First in Wiltshire and later at Wath, near York, he avidly recorded monuments up and down the land. He was particularly interested in the construction and layout of prehistoric funerary monuments.

After graduating in 1840 from Cambridge University, he was ordained at Salisbury in 1841. He held several livings in Wiltshire during which time he founded the Wiltshire Archaeology and Natural History Society. He then moved his growing family to Wath in Yorkshire in 1853 (Sebire 2003). He became a member of many British and French learned societies and was elected to the Society of Antiquaries of London and the Society of Northern Antiquities of Denmark. During the summer months he and his friend from his days at Cambridge, Sir Henry Dryden of Canons Ashby, near Daventry, examined and recorded megalithic monuments in various parts of the country. They had met at Cambridge and became lifelong friends. Dryden was the fourth baronet of Canons Ashby, Northamptonshire, and was a superb draughtsman and surveyor. Between them they visited all the major monuments known at the time, as far apart as Aberdeenshire and Wiltshire, Anglesey and Brittany. Some of these excursions were funded by the Society of Antiquaries of London to whom reports were made periodically.

Among W.C. Lukis' other interests was ecclesiastical history, and he published a treatise on Ancient Church Plate in 1845. He was also a regular contributor to the journals of the British Archaeological Association and other learned societies. He published many papers, some of which had particular relevance to Guernsey archaeology, e.g. 'Danish Cromlechs and Burial Customs compared with those of Brittany, the Channel Islands and Great Britain' (1864), 'On Cromlechs' (1864a), 'On a remarkable Chambered Long Barrow at Kerlescant, Carnac, Brittany', (1868) and 'On various Forms of Monuments, Commonly called Dolmens in Brittany, pointing out a Progress in their Architectural Construction with an Attempt to Reduce them to Chronological Order' which he presented to the International Congress of Prehistoric Archaeology, Norwich (1868a), to which his father accompanied him.

Hundreds of William's plans, sections and elevations of megalithic monuments in Scotland, England, Wales, Ireland, France, Algeria and the Netherlands survive in the archive at Guernsey Museum. The remainder of the Lukis and Dryden archives are housed variously at the Society of Antiquaries of London, the Department of Antiquities at the Ashmolean Museum in Oxford and Northampton Central Library. The Lukis and Dryden plans are very detailed and their level of accuracy is illustrated by comparison with plans drawn up using modern equipment. They were drawn to a standard format; stones in horizontal and vertical section were tinted pink, stones in elevation in grey and fallen stones in buff. The plans are also of value in showing where stones have been moved or lost since the 1880s. Interestingly, Lukis makes the following comment in one of his reports: *'There is not one among them that is in the condition in which it was left when the use for which it was erected ceased'* (Lukis 1884).

In 1880 a proposal was put to the Society of Antiquaries of London to publish all Lukis' and Dryden's plans of megaliths, and a brochure was circulated to invite subscriptions. Unfortunately only some were published, hampered at the time by a serious fire at the printers. R. J. C. Atkinson, in a paper written in honour of Stuart Piggott's sixty-fifth birthday, wrote: 'There can be no doubt if this project had been completed it would have ranked as one of the major archaeological publications of the nineteenth century, and would have earned for Lukis in the eyes of posterity a place no less occupied, say, by Sir John Evans or General Pitt-Rivers' (Atkinson 1976, 113). While there can be no argument about the value of this material, there is no doubt that William was very much influenced by his father's example and later collaboration. The majority of W.C. Lukis' collection of stone implements and pottery was sold to the British Museum just before his death.

Lukis' youngest son, Captain Francis du Bois Lukis, who had a career in the army, did not publish any of the work he carried out himself (particularly in Alderney), but his father sent in his notes of work in the Peak District to The Reliquary journal, which was published in Buxton in Derbyshire (Lukis 1868). It was also Francis who ensured that the entire museum collection was bequeathed, on his death and in accordance with his father's wishes, to the States of Guernsey.

Lukis had three daughters who, in keeping with the social norm at the time, probably did not have any formal schooling but in their own way made a contribution to megalithic studies. The eldest daughter, Louisa, was born in 1818. She married her cousin William Collings, who was Seigneur of Sark, in 1847. She inherited her father's interest in natural history, specialising in the collection of lichens, but she did illustrate some of her father's archaeological artefacts as well.

However it was his daughter Mary Anne, born in 1822, who devoted much of her time to illustrating her father's work. Amongst the written archives left by Lukis is a veritable museum on paper of archaeological drawings and watercolours of sites, locations and artefacts. Lukis' youngest daughter, Margaretta, was born in 1829. She also joined in family excursions to sites and drew some of them.

THE LUKIS FAMILY CONTRIBUTION TO MEGALITHIC STUDIES

F.C. Lukis and his family made an outstanding contribution to megalithic studies in the 19th century. In publication terms Lukis' seminal article was published in 1844 in the Archaeological Journal entitled 'Observations on the Primaeval Antiquities of the Channel Islands'. This was Lukis' first 'exposure' to the outside world, and through this article he successfully brought sites in Guernsey and the other Channel Islands to the attention of other antiquarians. In this article he describes a typical stratification in 'the northern district of the island of Guernsey' and illustrates this with a section drawing through a 'cromlech at L'Ancresse'. He then discusses the etymological roots of terms used to describe the monuments such as 'cromlech' and the local 'Pouquelaye'. He goes into some detail about the use of the term 'Druids Altar' and gives practical reasons why this hypothesis does not make sense:

> *The names "Druids Altar," "Temple des Druides," convey a meaning when applied to the cromlech, properly so called, and probably owe their origin to the generally received opinion, and the incorrect translation of the word cromlech, or "inscribed stone," affirmed by certain writers as disposed to permit the blood of the victims to flow from west to east all of which is mere conjecture and equally untenable* (Lukis 1844, 145).

He then describes the structural elements of the 'cromlechs' including the details of the excavations at La Varde on L'Ancresse. While discussing the ceramics associated with the tomb he writes (*ibid.* 150):

> "As several vessels bore the marks of use previous to interment, there can be no doubt that the most valuable and useful articles were deemed the most valuable and useful articles of the departed."

He even gives ethnographical parallels for the use of querns similar to those recovered from the excavation: *'They were simple rolled pebbles of various sizes, and were used as a pestle, or worked round the trough with the hand. This method is still observed among the natives of India and South America, where rice and other grain is to be pounded.'*

This work was acknowledged by both Daniel Wilson and John Lubbock, and later by Thoms in his English translation of Worsaae's *Antiquities of Denmark* (Thoms 1849). Daniel Wilson (1816-1892), a Scot, published *The Archaeology and Prehistoric Annals of Scotland* in 1851 and is thought to be the first person to use the word 'prehistory' (Daniel 1950, Bahn 1996). Wilson bemoaned the fact that all Scottish monuments had up to that time been ascribed to 'men from the north' (Scandinavia) whereas he considered (1851, xvi):

> "It is not a mere question of Northman or Dane and Celt and Saxon. It involves the entire chronology of the prehistoric British periods, and so long as it remains unsettled any consistent arrangement of our archaeological data into an historic sequence is impossible."

Although he did not meet J.J.A. Worsaae, who visited Edinburgh in 1846 to advise the Society of Antiquaries on the classification of their antiquities (Kehoe 1998, 16), Wilson catalogued the collections. He distinguished Stone and Bronze Age artefacts from Roman and Christian, and he exhorted the British Museum to do the same. In his major work *The Archaeology and Prehistoric Annals of Scotland*, Wilson quotes from Lukis' 1844 paper 'On the Primaeval Antiquities of the Channel Islands' (1851, 65), drawing comparisons with a Guernsey 'cromlech' and his description of Knocklegoil Cairn in Scotland.

Wilson's ideas were challenged by John Lubbock (1834-1913), later Sir John Lubbock, Lord Avebury, who published a seminal work, Pre-historic Times as illustrated by Ancient Remains and the Manners and Customs of Modern Savages (Lubbock 1865). Lubbock provided a synthesis of prehistory for the first time and his schemata of Palaeolithic and Neolithic were picked up by Lukis in 1868, just three years later, in his volumes on the implements of the Stone Age which form part of his *Collectanea*. He uses his knowledge of geology to identify the implements and publishes an illustration of five of the most typical forms. These included the exquisite polished battle axes which, some hundred and fifty years later, are still unique to Guernsey. Lukis senior went on to publish several other papers (Lukis 1846, 1846a, 1848a, 1848b, 1848c, 1849, 1850, 1853, 1854), which form only a small part of his written work as the volumes of the *Collectanea Antiqua* form the most comprehensive account of his work and contain the basic information from which the published papers are composed.

Georges Metivier, Guernsey's great romantic poet, dedicated a poem to his antiquarian friend and lover of megaliths at the end of his life:

Lukis

O Lukis, it is true! Young life's warm stream,
    Day after day, ebbs on, and on we go,
Now that each, gray with age, has dreamt his dream,
    To that calm land of souls where there's no woe.

For we *have* liv'd. Communion with the past,
    Home's tranquil joys, the love of ancient lore,
Kind words and looks to all, will prove, at last,
    That we are candidates for heav'ns bright door.

References

ATKINSON, R.J.C. (1976) Lukis, Dryden and the Carnac Megaliths, in: J.V.S. Megraw (ed.) *To Illustrate the*

Monuments: essays on archaeology presented to Stuart Piggott, London: Thames and Hudson. 112-24.

BAHN, P. (1996) *The Cambridge Illustrated History of Archaeology*, Cambridge: Cambridge University Press.

DANIEL, G.E. (1950) *A Hundred Years of Archaeology*, London: Duckworth.

GOSSELIN, J. (1813) An Account of some Druidical remains in the island of Guernsey, *Archaeologia* 17, 254-6.

LUBBOCK, J. (1865) *Pre-historic times, as illustrated by ancient remains, and the manners and customs of modern savages*, London: Williams and Norgate.

LUKIS, F.C. (1843) *Bircham Barrows*, Guernsey: Barbet.

LUKIS, F.C. (1844) Observations on the Primaeval Antiquities of the Channel Islands, *Archaeological Journal* 1, 144-152.

LUKIS, F.C. (1846) On the Cromlech of Du Tus, *Journal of the British Archaeological Association* 1, 25-29.

LUKIS, F.C. (1846a) On Sepulchral Graves in Guernsey, *Journal of the British Archaeological Association* 1, 305-308.

LUKIS, F.C. (1848) *Collectanea Antiqua* Vol. V, 21.

LUKIS, F.C. (1848a) On the Antiquities of Alderney, *Journal of the British Archaeological Association* 3, 1-15.

LUKIS, F.C. (1848b) On Stone Celts found in the Channel Islands, *Journal of the British Archaeological Association* 3, 127-128.

LUKIS, F.C. (1848c) On the Cromlech of L'Ancresse Common, *Journal of the British Archaeological Association* 3, 342-4.

LUKIS, F.C. (1849) On the Sepulchral Character of Cromlechs in the Channel Islands, *Journal of British Archaeological Association* 4, 323-337.

LUKIS, F.C. (1850) Communication on Hand-Bricks, *Archaeological Journal* 7, 175-6.

LUKIS, F.C. (1853) On a sepulchral Cave found in Guernsey, *Journal of the British Archaeological Society* 8, 64-67.

LUKIS, F.C. (Jun.) (1853) Observations on the Celtic Megaliths and the contents of Celtic Tombs, chiefly as they remain in the Channel islands, *Archaeologia* 35, 232-258.

LUKIS, F.C. (1854) On the Maenhir, *Journal of British Archaeological Association* 9, 426-428.

LUKIS, J.W. (1886) Note sur les anciens inhabitants et les monuments préhistoriques des Îles de Guernsey, Jersey, Aurigny, etc., *Bulletin Société D'Etudes Scientifiques de Finistère* 8, 9- 12.

LUKIS, J.W. (1888) Objets préhistoriques recueilles dans les monuments megalithiques des Îles de Guernsey, Jersey, Aurigny, etc., *Bulletin Société D'Etudes Scientifiques de Finistère* 10.

LUKIS, W.C. (1864) Danish Cromlechs and Burial Customs compared with those of Brittany, the Channel Islands and Great Britain, *Wiltshire Archaeology and Natural History Society Transactions* 3, 1-25.

LUKIS, W.C. (1864a) On Cromlechs, *Journal of the British Archaeological Association* 20, 228-237.

LUKIS, F.C. (1868) Archaeological notes made by Captain Francis Dubois Lukis, H.M.'s 64th Regiment during a visit to Buxton, Derbyshire, in 1865, *The Reliquary* 9, 81-87.

LUKIS, W.C. (1868) On a remarkable Chambered Long Barrow at Kerlescant, Carnac, Brittany, *Journal of the British Archaeological Association* 24, 40-44.

LUKIS, W.C. (1868a) On various Forms of Monuments, Commonly called Dolmens in Brittany, pointing out a Progress in their Architectural Construction with an Attempt to Reduce them to Chronological Order, *International Congress of Prehistoric Archaeology Norwich*, 218-232.

LUKIS, W.C. (1884) Report of Survey of certain megalithic monuments in Scotland Cumberland and Westmoreland, executed in summer 1884, *Proceedings of the Society of Antiquaries 1885 May 21*, 302-311.

MARSDEN, B. (1999) *The Early Barrow Diggers*, Stroud: Tempus.

OLIVER, S.P. (1870) Report on the Present State and Condition of Prehistoric Remains in the Channel Islands, *Journal of the Ethnographical Society of London* 11, 45-70.

SEBIRE, H.R. (2003) *Frederick Corbin Lukis of Guernsey: polymath and archaeologist, Unpublished Phd thesis*, University of Southampton.

THOMS, W. (1849) *The Primeaval Antiquities of Denmark by J.J.A. Worsaae. Translated and applied to the illustration of similar remains in England*, London: Parker.

WILSON, D. (1851) *The Archaeology and Prehistoric Annals of Scotland*, Edinburgh: Sutherland & Knox.

ANTIQUARIANS AT SWEDISH MEGALITHS

Karl-Göran SJÖGREN[*]

Department of archaeology and ancient history, Göteborg University, Box 200, S-40530 Göteborg, Sweden,
email: kg.sjogren@archaeology.gu.se

Abstract: Antiquarian interest in Swedish megaliths during the 16th and 17th centuries were embedded in the then current ideas derived from "gothic" myths and Icelandic sagas. In the early 18th century, as a result of broader interests in natural history, ethnographic traditions and social customs, information acquired by scholars travelling throughout the provinces, as well as that gathered by local priests or landowners, included mentions of megaliths. First investigations in the field began to provide accurate drawings and descriptions of monuments featured in notes and diaries. From the later 18th century onwards, well-documented excavations led to early classification of megaliths and to the interpretation of funerary practices such as seated burials, providing foundations for the emergence in the 19th century of "scientific" archaeology in which the study of megaliths played an important role.
Key words: Sweden, antiquarians, megaliths

Résumé: *La curiosité des antiquaires pour les mégalithes suédois durant les 16ème et 17ème siècles était enracinée dans les idées en cours à cette époque dérivées des mythes "gothiques" et des sagas islandaises. Au début du 18ème siècle, à la suite de l'élargissement de l'intérêt pour l'histoire naturelle, les traditions ethnographiques et les rites de la société, les informations acquises par les chercheurs durant leurs voyages à travers les provinces, ainsi que celles collectées par les curés ou les propriétaires, comprenaient des allusions aux mégalithes. Les premières fouilles de terrain commencèrent à fournir des dessins précis et des descriptions des monuments présentés dans des notes et journaux. Á partir de la fin du 18ème siècle, les fouilles bien documentées ont amené à un début de classification des mégalithes et à l'interprétation des pratiques funéraires (enterrement assis, présence d'hommes et de femmes) assurant les fondations de l'émergence au 19ème siècle d'une archéologie "scientifique" dans laquelle l'étude des mégalithes joua un rôle important.*
Mots-clés: *Suède, antiquaire, mégalithes*

In this paper I will present some examples of early antiquarian interest in Swedish megalithic tombs. The examples refer to the period up until c. 1850, i.e. when the new 'scientific' paradigm of how to study prehistory may be said to be have been established in Scandinavia. In Sweden, this topic has not been discussed much in archaeological literature. Recently, however, interest in the history of the discipline has risen considerably, and works on various aspects of it are starting to appear (Jensen 2002, Baudou 2004). Still, the early history of the study of megalithic tombs has only been treated rather partially, and mostly published in Swedish. This paper should therefore not be seen as a summary of the subject, but only as a series of examples centred on the area that I myself am most familiar with, namely western Sweden.

BACKGROUND

Three main types of megalith are usually distinguished in Scandinavia: dolmens, passage graves and gallery graves. Today, about 455 dolmens and passage graves are known in Sweden, but especially in the south a large number of tombs have been destroyed during the last two centuries. These tomb types were built in a rather short period c. 3300-3000 BC cal, i.e. the transition between the early and the middle Neolithic periods, in the cultural setting of the Funnel Beaker culture. The approximately 1500 gallery graves, on the other hand, were built mainly in the late Neolithic, c. 2400-1800 BC cal.

Swedish dolmens and passage graves have a very peculiar distribution and occur in two distinct types of landscape: close to the coast in Scania, Halland and Bohuslän, and in the inland area of Falbygden, Västergötland (Fig. 9.1). The gallery graves on the other hand have a very general distribution over most of southern Sweden, with a notable concentration in the south Swedish uplands, in present day Småland.

These diverse regions have also had different recent histories. Scania, Halland and Bohuslän only became Swedish provinces after 1658, after a long period of wars with Denmark. Before that, Scania and Halland belonged to Denmark while Bohuslän was part of Norway (the latter also being governed from Denmark since the late Medieval period). This sometimes very intense conflict also had a number of repercussions on early antiquarianism. Obviously, scholars were confined to working within the existing national boundaries. But, in addition to this, the work that they performed was part of a larger competitive ethos. It was important to demonstrate the glorious past, the important remains, the ancestral rights to the territory etc., and to show that "we" were already better than the Danes in the distant past.

The view of the past was, as in other European countries, shaped by reference to written sources such as the bible and various classical authors. From these, the peculiar "gothic" myth was constructed, which informed much of the early antiquarian work up until the 18th century. The idea of Scandinavia as the home of the Goths can be traced to the late medieval period and found its high point in the "Atlantica" of Olaus Rudbeckius, published 1679-1702. Even if few people went to similar extremes, passage graves were in fact often referred to as gothic

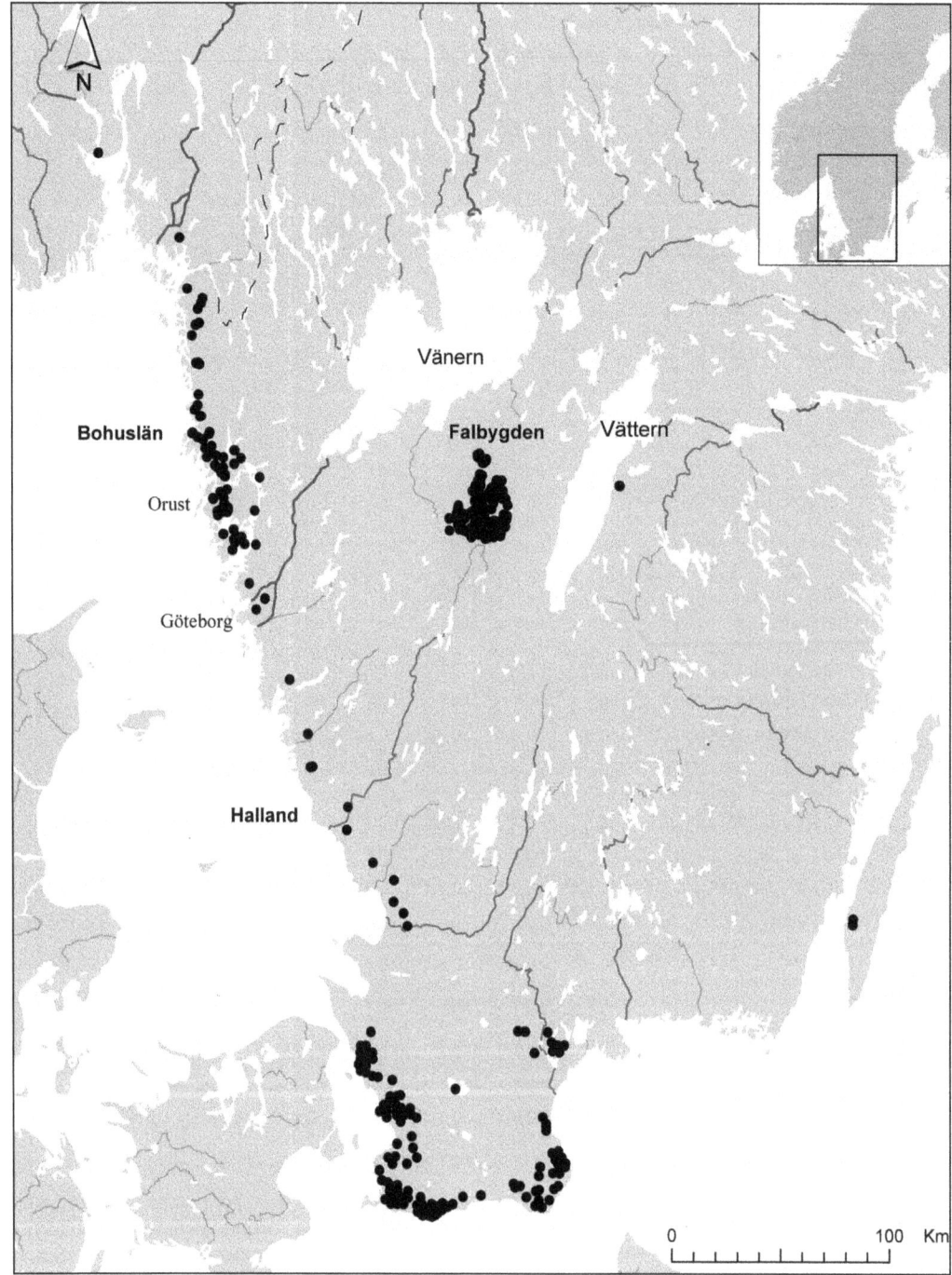

Fig. 9.1. The distribution of dolmens and passage graves in Sweden

tombs ("götiske grafvar") until the late 18th/early 19th century, when more descriptive terms like "T-cross grave", "cross grave" (T-korsgrav, T-korskummel, korskummel or halvkorsgrav), "cairn cave" (kummelgrotta) and later "passage grave" (gånggrift) came into use.

Another, partly conflicting, source of information was the Icelandic sagas, many of which were discovered and translated during the 17th century. From these, particularly from Snorri Sturlasson's "Heimskringla", a chronological system of burial customs was adopted (Hildebrand 1937:35ff, Jensen 2002). According to Snorri, with the arrival of Odin the custom of burning the dead and raising stones over them was introduced. Odin and the other pagan gods were thought to have arrived from Asia shortly before the birth of Christ. Snorri and later writers saw them not as gods but as important chiefs or heroes who had led their tribes to settle in Scandinavia. Later, after the burial of Frej at Uppsala, the custom of erecting barrows became common. Thus, there had been a "Barrow Age" (högålder) preceded by a "Cremation Age" (brännålder). These divisions were used, for instance, by Johannes Loccenius (1647) and also by Ole Worm in Denmark (Worm 1643). Somewhat later a third period was added, the "Cairn Age" (kummelåldern[1]). This was thought to have been the oldest period, preceding the Cremation Age. Some authors claimed this to be the age of giants, and megaliths were usually dated to this period. This chronological system was widely accepted until it was gradually replaced by the Three Age System in the decades around 1820-1840.

Another particular trait in Scandinavian antiquarianism is the amount of early state intervention. This took the form of legislation protecting the monuments (1666) or of creating institutions such as Riksantikvarien (National Antiquarian, 1630) and Antikvitetskollegiet (the College of Antiquities, 1666). The state also organised the first systematic attempts at surveying ancient monuments (Rannsakningar efter antiqviteter, 1667-1693). The survey would be carried out by parish priests, who were instructed to send in descriptive surveys to the National Antiquarian. Numerous descriptions came in, and here we find a number of descriptions of megalithic tombs, mainly gallery graves. They were usually referred to as heroes' graves or giants' graves, but sometimes also as dwarfs' houses. Unfortunately, most of the descriptions from the main passage grave area in Falbygden have been lost (Ståhle 1969, Ståhle & Stahre 1992).

For the Danish provinces, a very similar survey was organized by Ole Worm as early as the 1620s. In fact, these priestly records ("presteinberetninger") may have functioned as a model for the Swedish initiative. Only a few records of megalithic tombs survive, however, since most of the manuscripts were destroyed by fire in 1728.

THE EARLIEST REFERENCES

Although Saxo Grammaticus, in his "Gesta Danorum" (c. 1200), already refers to tombs built by giants from huge stone blocks, the first direct reference to Swedish megalithic tombs is found in the "Historia de gentibus septentrionalibus" by Olaus Magnus (1555). He comments on the "enormous stones that have been erected by gigantic force" and placed so "that they in a wonderful way are united into a high gate", and goes on to say that such stones are found particularly some 20 km from the town of Skara.[2] Although he views them as built by giants, he does not seem to think of them as burial places.

In 1647, Johannes Loccenius (1598-1677), professor of history and Roman law in Uppsala, describes ancient burial customs. He comments on giants' tombs built with large stone blocks, larger than any humans could have carried. He also mentions the unusual size of bones found in these tombs in support of the idea that giants had once lived there.[3] The comment on the size of the bones suggests that some excavations may have been done, but no records remain today.

Early national antiquarians, such as Johannes Bureus, Johan Hadorph and Johan Peringskiöld, made numerous journeys around the country to record ancient monuments. Since they were mainly interested in runic inscriptions, barrows and written documents, only a few comments regarding megalithic tombs can be found in their travel diaries. One example is found in two gallery graves at Hällekis in Västergötland, already mentioned by Loccenius 1647. They were described by Hadorph 1673 in an account of his travels with King Karl XI on his "Eriksgata".[4] He refers to these tombs as those of the giant Hälle and his wife Kisa (Jensen 2002:219).

Not all megalithic tombs were interpreted in this way, however. The idea of chamber tombs, particularly gallery graves, as houses once inhabited by dwarfs or trolls was also common, as indicated by the names given to many of them, such as the Dwarf's House (Dvärgahuset) or the Troll's Cottage (Trollastugan).

Another common idea was that of royal burial, usually derived from place names. One example is that of "Ragvald's grave" in Karleby, probably the largest passage grave in Scandinavia. According to tradition, this was the burial place of Ragvald Knaphövde, mentioned in early sources as having been murdered in Karleby during his Eriksgata through Västergötland, probably around 1126.

These early accounts consist only of descriptions, and no drawings are known. Neither do we have any reports of excavations from this time, but from the end of the 17th century we have the first accounts of finds from megalithic tombs.[5] These consist of flint daggers and axes, found in a few gallery graves in Bohuslän, Småland and Västergötland (Jensen 2002, Sjögren 2003). Rudbeck comments on these daggers in his *Atlantica*, and views them as used by ancient priests for circumcision or ritual hair cutting (Jensen 2002).

In view of the great interest in ancient history during this period, the direct references to megalithic tombs are

---

[1] Possibly by Jacob Wilde in his "Sueciae Historiae Pragmatica", from 1731, cf Hildebrand 1937:35.
[2] "...ofantliga stenar, som med jättekraft blifvit uppresta, dels lagda i horisontell ställning, så att de på ett underbart sätt äro förenade till en hög port; särskildt äro sådana stenar att se två dryga mil från staden Skara" (quuoted from the Swedish translation, Magnus 1982:66).
[3] "...och synes gå utöfver menniskio styrkio, at slika kunnat hopbäras af andra menniskior, än Jättar. Detta samma synes klarligen af några grafvars beliggenhet och owanliga längd; såsom och utaf de i jorden fundna bens ogemena storlek". (Quoted from the swedish translation, Loccenius 1728:278).
[4] Since medieval Sweden was not really a united nation but rather a federation of provinces (landskap), early kings had to travel through the various landscapes and be acknowledged separately in each one according to a formalized procedure. This journey, called "Eriksgata" was still undertaken in the 17th century but had now only symbolic significance.
[5] Some excavations were made, but concerning other types of monuments. For instance, Hadorph and Peringskiöld made excavations at the Viking Age town of Birka, and Rudbeck investigated several Iron Age tombs in order to develop a dating method based on the growth rate of the topsoil (Jensen 2002).

surprisingly few and scattered. Instead, much energy was devoted to the study of later monuments such as runic stones and large monuments that could be connected to early kings or other important persons. It must be noted, however, that megalithic tombs were not really distinguished as a category in this period. Instead, they were merged with other kinds of monumental constructions such as stone circles, ship settings etc, and referred to as giants' tombs (jättegrafvar), warrior graves (kämpegrafvar) or kings' graves.

THE 18TH CENTURY

In the 18th century, government interest in ancient remains dwindled considerably. At the same time, the earlier constructions of a heroic national past and the grand gothic myths were severely criticised. In this new rational and utilitarian era, speculation about prehistoric events based on monuments or artefacts was regarded with scepticism, and even ridiculed, by leading historians such as Olof von Dalin (1747) and Sven Lagerbring (1769). Also, earlier ideas about giants and dwarfs as early inhabitants of the area were gradually abandoned.

While state activity declined, antiquarian activity continued on a more private and decentralised level. Priests were still very active, but now academics and private landowners also made important contributions. One example is Johan Oedman, the parish priest in Tanum, Bohuslän. In his account of Bohuslän about ten megalithic tombs, mainly dolmens, are described (Oedman 1746). In his view, they were either sacrificial altars (offeraltare) or animal pens (dyrhus), while no mention is made of giants.

One important goal was now to increase knowledge of the nation for the sake of economic utility. With this in mind, a number of general descriptions of different provinces were made (ex Oedman 1746, Tidgren 1787, Bexell 1811). This was also the motivation for the travels in various provinces made by Carl von Linné and his pupils. Linné wrote detailed accounts, describing natural resources, fauna, flora, agriculture etc, but he also took an interest in history, so we get a few glimpses of ancient monuments. For instance, in his travels in western Sweden (1747) he describes the passage graves 'stora och lilla Hjelms rör' in Falköping.[6]

On a more local level, a large number of parish descriptions were made. If we take Västergötland as an example, these were made by parish priests according to a common plan in order to produce a complete description of the province. The original initiative came from Jacob Faggott. Sven Wilskman, teacher at the priest seminary in Skara, sent out a letter to the priests in 1749. The descriptions were supposed to include all kinds of economic and ethnographic information, but also ancient monuments, remarkable finds, local historical traditions etc. The project was never fully realised, but a large number of manuscripts did come in. These are of very variable quality, but a few of them contain very detailed and valuable information. For instance the manuscript by Thure Ljunggren from 1784, on the parishes of Slöta and Karleby in central Falbygden, is highly informative (Sandberg 1964). It was also one of the few published at the time (Ljunggren 1798). He described 10 passage graves from Karleby, giving details of construction, location and even sketch plans with measurements.

From some of these parish descriptions, it has been possible to estimate the number of tombs destroyed since the late 18th century. It turns out that, in contrast to many other megalithic regions, the passage graves in Falbygden have not suffered very much from the agricultural expansion of the 19th and 20th centuries, since only some 10-20 % of them seem to have disappeared (Sjögren 2003).

PER THAM, THE LAST RUDBECKIAN

Per Tham (1737-1820) is one of the more peculiar figures of Swedish antiquarianism (Schiller 1930, Nordbladh 2002). Born of wealthy parents, he made a career at the royal court and became a member of the parliament. However, in later life he more or less withdrew to his large estates in Dala and Dagsnäs, in his home province of Västergötland. Here, he dedicated himself to his own interests, such as managing his estates and sponsorship of various cultural projects. Among others, the poet Thomas Thorild was one of his beneficiaries.

Tham was a man of many and varied interests such as politics, economy and agrarian reform, but also a firm believer in the grand gothic myths outlined in the previous century. However, there was one big difference: according to Tham, it was not Uppsala and other places in eastern Sweden, but the areas around his home and his estates in Västergötland that were mentioned in early historic sources. This was the original home of the Goths, and where the Swedish kingdom had originated. He believed that Odin had lived on the eastern side of the Hornborga lake, just opposite Dagsnäs, and even that his own ancestry could be traced back to ancient Asa gods. The argument for this was that his mother's family had roots in Åsa parish in Småland. He expressed these views in several publications.[7] Apart from piecing together support for his ideas from various literary sources, Tham also made some field documentation of his own, in the form of drawings of ancient monuments. His most important contribution to archaeology, however, is his support of the fieldwork done by two others, Hilfeling and Sjöborg.

---

[6] Some of his comments may indicate that he also performed some sort of excavation in order to test Rudbecks dating method, cf. above.

[7] Such as "Göthiska monumenter" 1794, "Anteckningar under och i anledning av en resa från Westergötland till Stockholm" 1797, and "Politiska anteckningar" 1799.

Since passage graves in his view were gothic and dated from the oldest period, "Kummelåldern", they acquired a particular importance for him. It is interesting to note that passage graves were now classified as a separate category, called gothic tombs or T-cross graves, not only by Tham and Hilfeling but also by other authors. Some terminology for the details of construction was also developed. For instance the "key stone" (the innermost roof block on the passage) is described by Hilfeling on many graves, a term that is still with us today.

For Tham it was of great significance that the "gothic tombs", i.e. the passage graves, were concentrated in the Falbygden area, something that came about as a result of Hilfeling's surveys. Dolmens, on the other hand, were treated as something very different and were usually seen as temples, altars or offering tables from a much later period. This view was to persist for a long time, and was still expressed by scholars such as Sven Nilsson in the middle of the 19th century.

THE CONDUCTEUR CARL GUSTAF GOTTFRID HILFELING

Although Tham made some drawings himself, one of his main sources was C.G.G Hilfeling (1740-1823). This remarkable person could be called the first professional field archaeologist in Scandinavia, doing surveys, drawings and even some excavations (Schiller 1930, Nordbladh 1997, 2002). Born in Norrköping, he learned to draw in his early years but started out as a goldsmith. Eventually, he got employment as a draughtsman from a Danish historian, Jacob Langebek. Between 1767 and 1787 he made numerous antiquarian travels in Denmark and Scania, and was sometimes employed by the Danish state. Manuscripts and drawings from these journeys are kept in the national library in Copenhagen (Noreen 1964). Among other things, they contain some of the first documentation of the famous Bronze Age cairn at Kivik in Scania.

In 1788 he was employed by Per Tham to do similar work in Sweden, and worked for him for several years, up until 1801. Initially he travelled mainly in Västergötland and Bohuslän, but later he extended the journeys to Småland, Öland and Gotland. A large number of diaries and drawings are now kept in the Royal Library and in the archive of the National Board of Antiquities in Stockholm. Only some of this material was published in his lifetime, mainly by Tham (1794) who published drawings from Bohuslän. Some drawings were also published by Sjöborg (1822-1830). Later, some additional material was published (Hilfeling 1942a, 1942b, Gislestam 1994-95).

In general, Hilfeling's drawings are accurate and well made. His diaries contain detailed descriptions of megalithic tombs as well as other types of monuments, and also many anecdotes and comments on the people he met. Usually, his comments on the monuments are sober, and he refrains from the far-fetched speculations of his employer. In Figure 9.2, a comparison is shown between his drawing of the tomb Hjelmars rör in Falköping and a photograph of the same grave from 1932 (Fig. 9.2). Hilfeling's many travels in different regions also placed him in a position to make geographical comparisons, and he was the first to note the peculiar distribution of Swedish passage graves (see Fig. 9.1).

THE FIRST INVESTIGATION: DALA GÄRDE 1788

As far as I know, the first more or less systematic excavation of a Swedish megalithic tomb was made by Hilfeling. The investigation was made in 1788, the first year of Hilfeling's employment by Tham, when a passage grave at Dala gärde in Falbygden was excavated. The village of Dala was one of those owned by Tham, and the grave was located on his property. Unfortunately there is no report preserved, but we do have drawings in plan and profile by Hilfeling. It was later published by Tham in his "Politiska anteckningar" (Tham 1799: 56) and by Sjöborg (Sjöborg 1822:100, cf. also Sahlström 1932:4, Persson & Sjögren 2001:16).

The drawings show the layout of the tomb, but they also give some hints as to how Hilfeling and Tham interpreted the burial customs (Fig. 9.3). On the profile, sitting skeletons are indicated in a sort of X-ray view, and a comment reads: "on the bottom were bones unburned: normal size: no Monuments".[8] The view that the bodies had been buried in sitting position was also expressed by Tham (1799). In a comment on the drawing he says that "This plate shows, in my view, one of our oldest tombs of Gylfe before the arrival of Odin; ... you were set down in the mound as the bones show at a-a, – and they did not lie alongside like newer bodies"[9] (Tham 1799:56). The view that megalithic tombs had been constructed by giants was still current, but Tham and Hilfeling preferred to see them as indicating the heroic gothic past of Sweden, hence the emphasis on the normal size of the bones. The remark on the lack of "monuments" would indicate the lack of any interesting artifacts. A further interesting conclusion drawn by Hilfeling is that he sees them as family tombs (familiaegrafvar, cf. Sahlström 1932:4).

ODIN'S GRAVE AT AXVALLA

Very similar conclusions were to be drawn a few years later in connection with the excavation of another tomb, at Axvalla 1805. This was probably the first Swedish rescue excavation, since it was occasioned by the transformation of the Axvalla heath into a military training ground. In total, five megaliths and a few other monuments were

---

[8] "På botn fanns ben obrända: vanligt stora: inga Monumenter".

[9] "Denna taflan visar, efter min tanka, våra äldsta eller Gylfes grafvar innan Odins hitkomst; ... Man sattes i högen som benen utvisa vid a,a, – och de lågo icke längs efter som nymodigare lik".

Fig. 9.2. Hilfeling's drawing of the passage grave Hjelmars rör in 1789, compared to a photo of the monument from 1932

levelled, but one of them, the so-called Odin's grave, became famous since quite a detailed documentation was made. The work was led by an army Captain, Anders Lindgren, who applied his military survey training to the excavation. Thus he made both plans and cross-sections, showing the layout of the tombs, inner partitions in the chamber, as well as the positions of individual skeletons (Fig. 9.4). He also calculated the volume and weight of the roof blocks and of the surrounding mound, something which had no precedent and would not usually be done even in later excavations. He points out clearly that no finds of metal were made in any of the five excavated tombs.

Lindgren was a man with scientific interests and a member of the Royal Society of Arts and Sciences in Göteborg (Kungl. Vetenskaps- och Vitterhets- Samhället i Göteborg). In the proceedings of this society he published two accounts (Lindgren 1806, 1808). Compared to earlier writers, his text is remarkably clear and free from

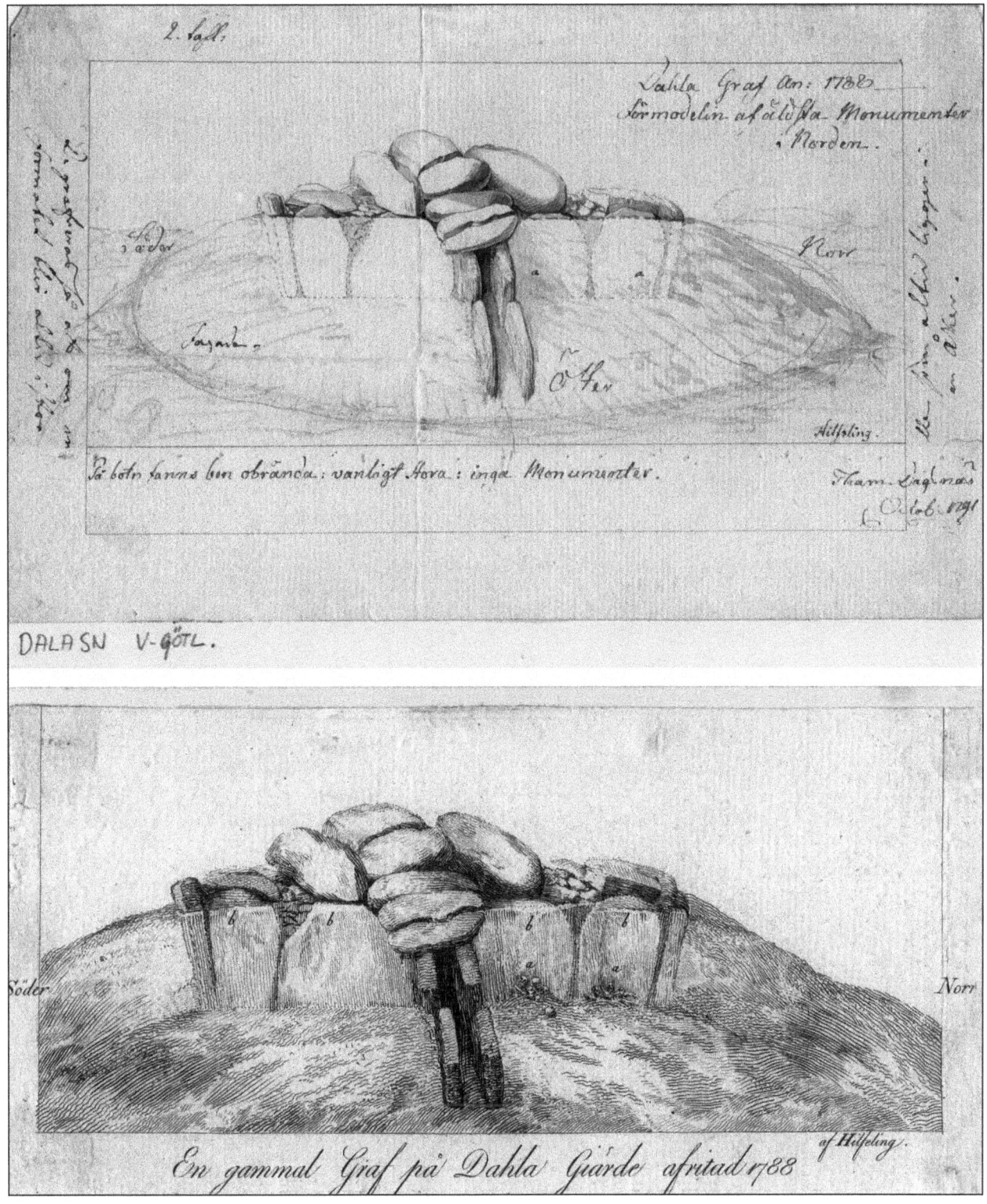

Fig. 9.3. Hilfeling's drawing of the passage grave at Dala gärde, as redrawn in 1791 (above), compared to the etching by Elias Martin published by Tham in 1799 (below)

speculations. He describes clearly the compartments in the chamber and notes the position of human bones and of artefacts in relation to them. He accepts the theory put forward by Hilfeling and Tham, that bodies had been buried in a sitting position. Further, he notes that bones from both children and adults occur. He also believes that both sexes were interred, men in the northern end of the chamber and women in the southern. This idea was not based on the bones themselves but on the distribution of certain finds (amber beads and flint knives). All this leads him to the conclusion that this and other similar tombs were burial places for kin groups ("Slägt-grifter").

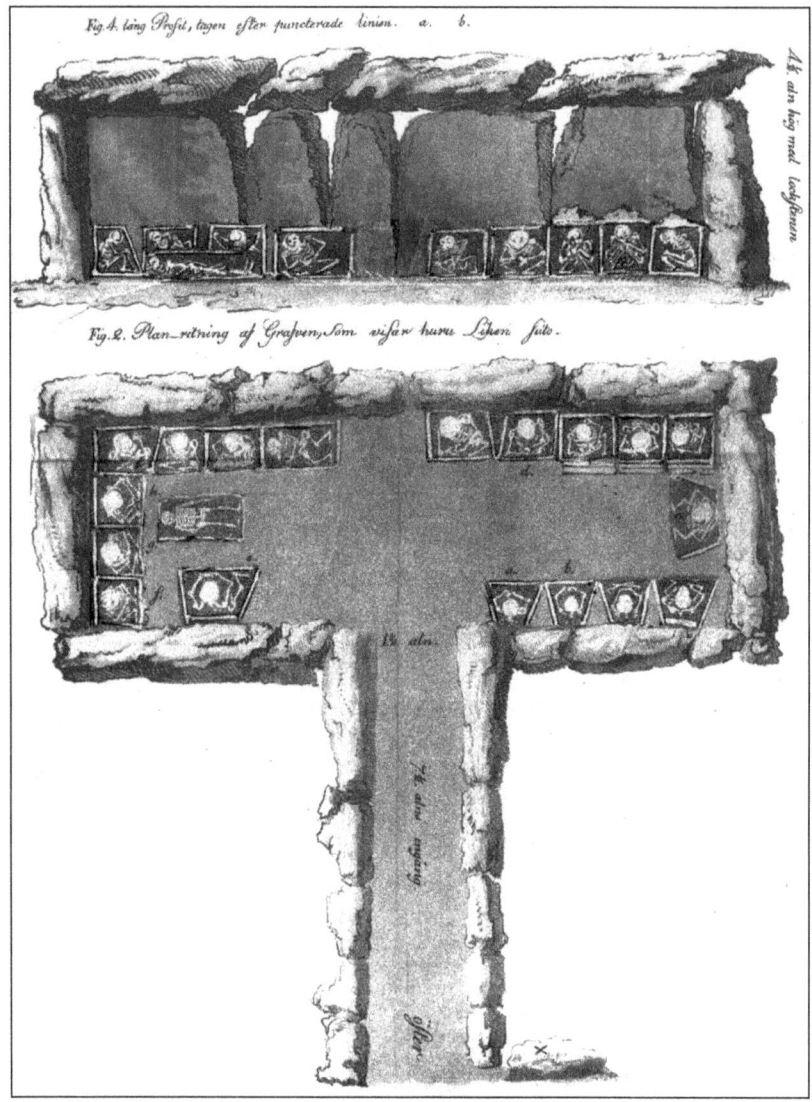

Fig. 9.4. Drawing of Odin's grave by Lindgren 1805.
Etching made from Lindgren's original

The excavation of Odin's grave was probably one of the best documented for its time. It also became quite well known outside Sweden, since an account with drawings was published in French very quickly by Malte-Brun[10] (1807).

It is not clear what relation Lindgren had to Tham and Hilfeling, but both of them were still alive and active at that time. A letter from Lindgren to Tham in July 1806 shows that they were in contact at least after the excavation, and before the 1808 publication. The similarity of the interpretations leads us to speculate that they had influenced Lindgren, and perhaps visited the excavation, which was situated only some 10 km from Dagsnäs. Sjöborg (1822), on the other hand, suggests that Hilfeling had not been aware of the excavation, and complains that no antiquarian expert had been consulted. At the same time, Lindgren seems to be quite independent in much of his reasoning, and his sources of inspiration remain largely unknown.[11]

ON THE VERGE OF 'SCIENTIFIC' ARCHAEOLOGY

In the first half of the 19th century, the study of ancient times was transformed into what we now more or less can recognise as the discipline of archaeology. This includes a number of things: the development of institutions, museum collections, learning networks, conferences etc.,

---

[10] Information and drawings came via Martin Friedrich Arendt, who had visited Tham at Dagsnäs. Tham had obtained copies of the drawings from Lindgren in 1806. Arendt, known as "the wandering antiquarian" travelled for many years on foot through Europe from Italy to northern Norway, visiting and documenting all sorts of antiquities and monuments.

[11] The published text contains a number of footnotes with many and varied literary references, but it seems that these have all been added by the editor. The text itself is virtually free from references to other authors.

all of which formed the basis of the new comparative method advocated by people like Thomsen, Nilsson and Worsaae.

Still, a few people continued to work in the older tradition. Among them were J.F. Mellin and Nils Salander, two priests who published descriptions of their parishes in the well established tradition of the 18th century (Salander 1811, Mellin 1812). The more ambitious of the two was Mellin, who had made excavations of two tombs in Hångsdala in Västergötland; a passage grave and a gallery grave. The results were similar to the earlier excavations. He notes a number of details in the chamber, such as stratigraphy, the occurrence of inner partitions, lack of metal implements etc. Like Hilfeling he comments on the normal size of the bones, and he views them as family tombs dating from "kummelåldern". Even later, the ethnographer Nils Månsson Mandelgren travelled the country around the middle of the century, recording nearly everything he saw; among his manuscripts, now in Lund, there are many drawings of megalithic tombs (cf. Axelsson & Sjögren 2000), some of them of quite good quality.

Among them may also be mentioned Nils Henrik Sjöborg (1767-1838), another of Tham's protégés. Like Hilfeling he was sponsored by Tham to make antiquarian journeys, mainly in southern Sweden. Later he became professor of history in Lund and an antiquarian in Stockholm. Among his interests was the classification of monuments (Sjöborg 1797, 1815) using a terminology largely taken from Icelandic sagas. His main work (Sjöborg 1822-1830) is descriptive, containing a number of drawings made by his own hand as well as copies of others. Unfortunately his drawings are of rather poor quality, and some seem to be made from memory rather than in the field. His interpretations are entirely within the old school, using classical and Icelandic authors as authorities.

Sjöborg was not alone, however. In fact, the years around 1800 saw a marked revival of the interest in antiquities, witnessed for instance by the foundation of the 'Gothic society' (Götiska förbundet) in 1811. The main focus of the interest in ancient monuments was now in Lund. Here, a number of people made important contributions, such as Magnus Bruzelius and Sven Nilsson. The cultural environment had now changed radically and included also scholars such as C.J. Thomsen in Copenhagen, and we may talk of a 'cultural Scandinavianism', preceding the later political one (Hildebrand 1937). It was in this productive environment that the old saga-based periodisation was replaced by a three-age system, based more on find contexts, systematic comparison and ethnographic analogy than on literary sources.

Sven Nilsson's (1787-1883) contribution to archaeology is fairly well known and will not be discussed here. Magnus Bruzelius (1786-1855), on the other hand, has been largely forgotten although he was one of the more independent and empirically oriented scholars of his time (Hildebrand 1937: 315ff, Gräslund 1987). He was originally a natural scientist, employed as docent in chemistry at Lund University. Later, he entered the priesthood and worked as a parish priest in Löderup in eastern Scania from 1824 on.

He took a great interest in archaeology and published a series of works in 1816-23. Among them is one of the most important of the early excavations of megalithic tombs, at Åsahögen in Scania (Bruzelius 1822). The finds were abundant and consisted of human and animal bones, amber beads, pottery and stone artefacts. He took care to employ experts in treating the finds; thus the anatomist Arvid Herman Florman determined the human remains and Sven Nilsson the animal bones.[12] He gives a thorough description of the excavation, noting details about construction, stratigraphy and the position of particular artefacts as well as of human and animal bones. Notably, this is the first Swedish tomb with finds of decorated TRB pottery (Fig. 9.5). From the osteological analyses by Florman, it is clear that both men and women are buried, as well as children and adults. Bruzelius draws the conclusion that the tomb had been used in two different periods, represented by two layers in the chamber, by families belonging to a kin group.

As regards dating and interpretation, Bruzelius may be said to have a foot in both camps. He is very clear about the importance of the lack of metals, and uses the term "Stone Age" instead of "Cairn Age". On the other hand, in other passages he refers to the immigration of Odin as a historical fact, dating the introduction of cremation burial. On the whole, however, he does not treat historical sources as providing the final answer, but speaks also of a period before them and beyond their reach.

On the interpretative level he also introduces a new idea, probably for the first time in Scandinavia, namely the idea of megalithic tombs as ossuaries, places where already skeletised bones had been placed. In support he quotes a number of ethnographic examples, among others Cook's description of burial customs in "Otahiti".[13] This idea was to become very influential in later writings, and Bror Emil Hildebrand, for instance, follows it closely in his discussion of the passage graves in Slöta and Luttra which he excavated in 1863 (Hildebrand 1864).

COMMENTS

The examples presented here give only a rough outline of antiquarian activity in connection with Scandinavian

---

[12] Like Bruzelius, Nilsson was originally a natural scientist, and had published a number of works in zoology. Florman was a leading anatomist and osteologist in his time, and may be said to have founded the craniometric tradition in Scandinavian archaeology, which was later taken up by his pupils Sven Nilsson and Anders Retzius, and followed up by Gustaf Retzius, son of Anders Retzius.

[13] In a letter to Tham in 1806, Lindgren actually suggests a similar idea. In the 1808 paper, this is not mentioned, however.

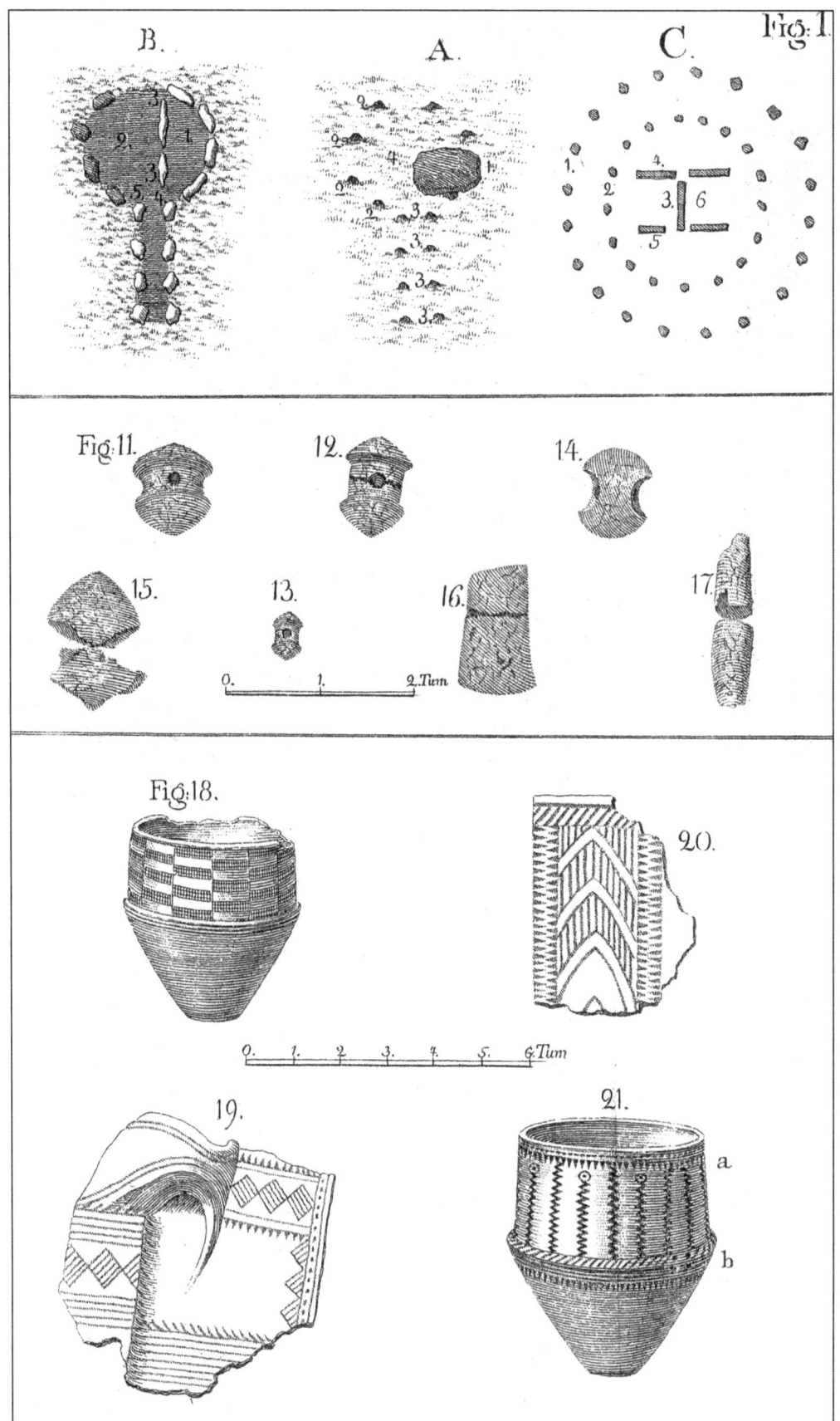

Fig. 9.5. Drawing of Åsahögen (Bruzelius 1822). 1A and B show the tomb before and during excavation; 1C is another tomb, at Fjelkinge in Scania; his Figs 11-17 show amber beads and 18-21 TRB pottery from Åsahögen. Note the two complete hanging vessels, now known to be very characteristic of Scanian megalithic pottery

megaliths. Many questions remain to be explored before we can begin to see what the limitations were and what the lasting impact of antiquarianism may have been, for instance on the emerging 'scientific' archaeology of the 19th century. In many accounts, this impact is denied more or less completely, emphasising the heroism and geniality of pioneers such as Thomsen (ex. Klindt-Jensen 1975, Gräslund 1987).

Certainly many of the ideas put forward by people like Tham seem to us very strange and far-fetched, and the dependence on literary sources was a major limitation. At the same time, many of the detailed interpretations of sites like Dala gärde and Axvalla are not very different from what we are saying today. In the early 19th century, these would probably have been very valuable parts of the empirical basis for the formulation of the new paradigm. Influence works on different levels, and even if the 'top' level of interpretation may have seemed speculative or even crackpot, the impact on other levels may have been considerable.

References

AXELSSON, T. & SJÖGREN, K.-G. (2000) "Han är oförskämd och obehaglig att se och höra". Nils Månsson Mandelgrens teckningar av gånggrifter på Falbygden. *Falbygden* 54, pp. 33-45.

BAUDOU, E. (2004) *Den nordiska arkeologin – historia och tolkningar*. Kungl. Vitterhets- historie- och antikvitets- akademien. Almqvist & Wiksell International, Stockholm.

BEXELL, S.P. (1927) [1811] *Hallands historia och beskrifning*. Halmstad.

BRUZELIUS, M. (1822) Nordiska Fornlemningar från Skåne. *Iduna IX*, pp. 285-333.

DALIN, O. von (1747) *Svea rikes historia*, del 1. Stockholm.

GRÄSLUND, B. (1987) *The Birth of Prehistoric Chronology. Dating methods and dating systems in nineteenth-century Scandinavian archaeology*. New Studies in Archaeology. Cambridge University Press: Cambridge.

HILDEBRAND, B. (1937) *C.J, Thomsen och hans lärda förbindelser i Sverige 1816-1837. Bidrag till den nordiska forn- och hävdaforskningens historia*. KVHAA Handlingar 44:1-2. Uppsala.

HILDEBRAND, B.E. (1864) Berättelse om antiqvariska undersökningar i Vestergötland år 1863. *Antiqvarisk Tidskrift för Sverige* I, sid 255-283.

HILFELING, C.G.G. (1942a) [1788] ANMÄRKNINGAR UTI ANTIQVITETEN på en 8 dagars resa i Westergötlands fahlbygd. *Västergötlands Fornminnesförenings Tidskrift* 1942, pp. 70-85.

HILFELING, C.G.G (1942b) [1798] Dagbok. Hållen under resan til Skåne och Dannemark år 1798. *Västergötlands Fornminnesförenings Tidskrift* 1942, pp. 85-90.

KLINDT-JENSEN, O. (1975) *A history of Scandinavian archaeology*. Thames & Hudson, London.

JENSEN, O.W. (2002) *Forntid i historien. En arkeologihistorisk studie av synen på forntid och forntida lämningar från medeltiden till förupplysningen*. GOTARC Serie B nr 19. Institutionen för arkeologi, Göteborgs universitet.

LAGERBRING, S. (1769) *Svea rikes historia*, del 1. Stockholm.

LINDBLAD, A. (1935) [1790] *Beskrifning öfver Gökhems församling*. Falbygdens Hembygds- och Fornminnesförening, Falköping.

LINDGREN, A. (1806) *Gbg Wettenskaps- och Witterhets Samh. Handlingar Witterhetsafd.* V, pp. 82-84.

LINDGREN, A. (1808) *Ytterligare underrättelse om en på Axevalla hed upptäckt Forngrift*. Götheborgska Wettenskaps- och Witterhets Samhällets Handlingar. Wettenskapsafd. V, pp. 87-103.

LINNE, C. von (1747) *Wästgöta-Resa*. Stockholm.

LJUNGGREN, T. (1798) Karleby socken: ålderdoms minnesmärken. *Skara månadsskrift*, pp. 37-41.

LOCCENIUS, J. (1647) *Antiquitatum sweo-gothicarum libri tres*. Stockholm.

LOCCENIUS, J. (1728) *Swenske och göthiske gamle handlingar*. Stockholm.

MAGNUS, O. (1982) [1555] *Historia om de nordiska folken*. Gidlund, Stockholm.

MALTE-BRUN, C. (1807) Notice d'un ancien tombeau de Westrogothie. *Annales des voyages, de la géographie et de l'histoire*, T. 1. Paris.

MELLIN, J.F. (1812) *Beskrifning öfver Hångsdala församling i Skaraborgs län*. Stockholm.

NORDBLADH, J. (1997) Conducteuren C.G.G Hilfeling och hans samtid. Åkerlund, Bergh, Nordbladh & Taffinder (ed): *Till Gunborg. Arkeologiska samtal*, pp. 527-538. SAR. Stockholm Archaeological Reports. Nr 33.

NORDBLADH, J. (2002) How to organize oneself within history: Per Tham and his relation to antiquity at the end of the 18th century. *Antiquity 76*, pp. 141-150.

NORDBLADH, J. (2004) Sjöborg, Nils Henrik. Karlsson, Å (ed.): *Svenskt biografiskt lexikon*, no 158. Sjöborg-Skoog. Stockholm.

NOREEN, S.E. (1964) Rare Prospector. Om antikvitetstecknaren C.G.G Hilfeling. *Ale 2*, pp. 1-15.

OEDMAN, J. (1983) [1746] *Chorographia Bahusiensis Thet är: Bahus-Läns Beskrifning*. Bohusläningen, Stockholm.

PERSSON, P. & SJÖGREN K.-G. (2001) *Falbygdens gånggrifter. Undersökningar 1985 till 1998*. GOTARC ser C nr 34. Institutionen för arkeologi, Göteborgs universitet.

RICHARDSON, J. (1987) [1752] *Hallandia antiqua et hodierna, thet är Hallands, et af Götha rikets landskaper, historiska beskrifning*. Stockholm.

SALANDER, N. (1811) *Beskrifning öfver Åsleds församling*. Stockholm.

SANDBERG, E. (ed) (1964) Thure Ljunggrens beskrivning över Slöta pastorat år 1784. *Falbygden 19*, pp. 141-166.

SCHILLER, H. (1930) *En originell herre*. Stockholm.

SJÖBORG, N.H. (1797) *Inledning till Kännedom af Fäderneslandets Antiquiteter*. Lund.

SJÖBORG, N.H. (1815) *Försök till en Nomenklatur för Nordiska Fornlemningar*. Stockholm.

SJÖBORG, N.H. (1822-30) *Samlingar för Nordens fornälskare 1-3*. Lund.

SJÖGREN, K.-G. (2003) *"Mångfalldige uhrminnes grafvar..."Megalitgravar och samhälle i Västsverige*. GOTARC ser B nr 27, Coast to coast-books nr 9. Dep. Of archaeology, Göteborg university.

STÅHLE, C.I. (ed) (1969) *Rannsakningar efter antikvititeter. Bd 2*. KVHAA fristående monografier.

STÅHLE, C.I. & STAHRE, N.-G. (eds) (1992) *Rannsakningar efter antikvititeter. Bd 3*. KVHAA fristående monografier.

THAM, P. (1794) *Göthiska Monumenter*. Stockholm.

THAM, P. (1797) *Anteckningar under och i anledning av en resa från Westergötland till Stockholm*.

THAM, P. (1799) *Politiska anteckningar*. Skara.

TIDGREN G. (1787) *Vestergötlands historia och beskrifning*. Stockholm.

WORM, O. (1643) *Monumentorum Danicorum libri sex*. København.

www.ingramcontent.com/pod-product-compliance
Lightning Source LLC
Chambersburg PA
CBHW061549010526
44115CB00023B/2988